Witches, Ogres, and the Devil's Daughter

A C. G. JUNG FOUNDATION BOOK

The C. G. Jung Foundation for Analytical Psychology is dedicated to helping men and women grow in conscious awareness of the psychological realities in themselves and society, find healing and meaning in their lives and greater depth in their relationships, and live in response to their discovered sense of purpose. It welcomes the public to attend its lectures, seminars, films, symposia, and workshops and offers a wide selection of books for sale through its bookstore. The Foundation also publishes *Quadrant*, a semiannual journal, and books on Analytical Psychology and related subjects. For information about Foundation programs or membership, please write to the C. G. Jung Foundation, 28 East 39th Street, New York, NY 10016.

MARIO JACOBY
VERENA KAST
INGRID RIEDEL

Witches, Ogres, and the Devil's Daughter

Encounters with Evil
in Fairy Tales

Translated by MICHAEL H. KOHN

SHAMBHALA
Boston & London
1992

Shambhala Publications, Inc.
Horticultural Hall
300 Massachusetts Avenue
Boston, Massachusetts 02115

Shambhala Publications, Inc.
Random Century House
20 Vauxhall Bridge Road
London SW1V 2SA

9 8 7 6 5 4 3 2 1

First Edition

Printed in the United States of America on acid-free paper
⊛
Distributed in the United States by Random House, Inc., in
Canada by Random House of Canada Ltd., and in the
United Kingdom by Random Century Group

Library of Congress Cataloging-in-Publication Data
Böse im Märchen. English
    Witches, ogres, and the devil's daughter/Mario Jacoby,
Verena Kast, Ingrid Riedel.
        p. cm.
    Translation of: Böse im Märchen.
    "A C.G. Jung Foundation book"—ISBN 0-87773-613-8
(pbk.)
        1. Fairy tales—History and criticism.
2. Psychoanalysis and folklore. 3. Polarity (Religion)
I. Jacoby, Mario. II. Kast, Verena, 1943—
III. Riedel, Ingrid, 1935—   . IV. Title.
GR550.B6313 1991   91-52524
398'.042—dc20   CIP

Contents

v

Preface

Is it really the case, as is often urged, that fairy tales are sometimes so gruesome that we should hesitate to let them fall into the hands of children, for whom they were never intended in the first place? Fairy tales are adult stories, told for life's critical times, liminal situations involving the utmost dangers, the direst trials, and transformation of the whole person through death and rebirth. However, the first phase of radical transformation is the one that leads from childhood to adulthood—puberty. Experience has often shown that children who know fairy tales have a better orientation in facing puberty's trials than those who have grown up without them. Could it be that children need an "initiation" into evil in order to get through it when the critical time comes?

My own initiation into evil continues to be a source of reflection for me. My time of fairy tale reading—from age eight to ten—coincided with the experience of the air raids of the Second World War. In the air-raid shelter, as the bombs were exploding all around, as fear arose in me for everything that then made up my world—my parents, my brothers and sisters, our house—I sat and read fairy tales, gruesome ones too, against the fear.

They helped me because they were conscious of evil, did not belittle or cosmeticize it, and nevertheless were able to pit stronger forces against it. They were in touch with evil and showed me saving powers that could break its spell. For I seemed to myself in those cellars to be under a spell, a spell of fear, which was almost more difficult to bear than the real danger. Fairy tales seemed to me at that time to be personal adepts for dealing with evil. I experienced them as protective powers, allied with me against chaos. They helped me to get through my fear, to keep my composure even when external danger and human panic prevailed around me. It was as if they showed me a more elevated, superior, and meaningful pattern of events and relationships in which, though evil had its place and time, it did not have the last word.

Fairy tales tell about critical encounters with evil and are intended for just such critical times. I experienced that as a child.

It is no accident that, in adult crises as well, fairy tales and fairy tale motifs can turn up again like lost keys and enter into consciousness. The archetypal motifs of fairy tales abound in the dreams of people who are under the pressure of acute suffering and seek psychotherapeutic treatment. Such people recount dreams whose structure and symbology unmistakably recall fairy tales. Such dreams are considered particularly significant. The dream material often closely resembles a fairy tale, and in the tale we often find a surprising suggestion for the solution of the dreamer's problem.

The connection between fairy tales and psychic processes and the attempt to understand fairy tales as suggestions for solving psychological problems is the common theme of the essays brought together in this book. The observations and reflections reported here all stem ultimately from psychotherapeutic practice, which, to the extent that it is based on C. G. Jung's depth psychology, deals primarily with analysands' dreams, their amplification, and their underlying archetypal structure, which fairy tales express. This kind of direct, practical, psychological way of working with fairy tales, particularly with evil in fairy tales, is what the essays in this volume seek to encourage.

The essays are arranged according to their inner content. In

Part One, the various ways of approaching fairy tales in depth psychology are described. Mario Jacoby introduces the *hermeneutical* approach of understanding and interpreting fairy tales as products of the creative imagination and the unconscious. The *thematic* approach is delineated in Verena Kast's essay "How Fairy Tales Deal with Evil," whose primary concern is understanding the function of evil within the developmental process of a fairy tale, frequently as a part of "that force that always seeks evil and always works good" (*Faust*). Next, "Methodological Remarks on Fairy Tale Interpretation" once more shows that fairy tales should not be conceived of and interpreted in terms of static symbolism but rather primarily in terms of their movement and development.

Part Two is composed of interpretations of exemplary individual fairy tales. Though it falls far shy of a comprehensive phenomenology of evil, nevertheless an attempt is made here to present typical examples of evil in fairy tales. Verena Kast finds in fairy tales the problem of repressed "giant affects," which is connected with sadomasochism, a common relationship pattern of our time. She also finds the very central contemporary problem of upsurge and upheaval of the feminine archetype. Further material on this problem is contained in my chapter on the Czech fairy tale "The Smith's Daughter Who Knew How to Hold Her Tongue." Its many-layered parallels lead us to suspect that the transformation in the feminine archetype is something affecting the entirety of Western culture. The particular concern here is the integration of split-off natural and demonized parts of ourselves into our general consciousness.

In Part Three, Mario Jacoby's essays on fairy tale motifs in psychotherapy are presented. Here the patients' problems are in the foreground. The point of departure is not the text of a fairy tale but patients' dreams, which nevertheless clearly constellate fairy tale themes, such as the sleep curse of Sleeping Beauty. The success or failure of an analysis can depend on whether we recognize the connection between the behavioral pattern of the patient and the fairy tale pattern that expresses the nature of the complex functioning within it, so that we are able to make use of the opportunities for solutions offered in equal measure by the dream and the fairy tale. Transference and countertransference also often occur in accordance with patterns that are vividly described in fairy tales and can be more fruitfully utilized in therapy if one takes into account the wisdom of the fairy tale. Here in the critical situation of therapy with psychologically disturbed people we find proof of the immediacy and relevance of fairy tales. They carry within them a fundamental knowledge handed down through the generations that can effectively broaden a therapist's possibilities.

The basic ideas for these fairy tale studies were set forth at a series of conferences of the Hofgeismar Evangelical Academy under the general title "Perspectives in Fairy Tale Research." Following a presentation at the first conference of the fruits of sociological research into fairy tales and of research into comparative symbology up to that time, in accordance with the interest of the participants, the focal point for the conferences of 1975 and 1976 was shifted to depth psychology. The remarks of Verena Kast and Mario Jacoby were presented in expanded form as lectures at the C. G. Jung Institute in Zurich in 1977.

I take pleasure in responding to the wishes of the large circle of those who attended the conferences and lectures by making this variety of contributions toward a depth-psychological interpretation of fairy tales available in one volume. It will perhaps be stimulating to encounter a number of methodologically distinct approaches toward the same objective: a discipline of fairy tale interpretation based on the broad vision of C. G. Jung.

All the authors owe rich inspiration to the groundbreaking studies of Marie-Louise von Franz, among which the most especially relevant for our theme are "The Problem of Evil in Fairy

Tales," "Bei der schwarzen Frau" (With the Black Woman),[2] and *Shadow and Evil in Fairy Tales.*[3]

Ingrid Riedel

NOTES

1. "The Problem of Evil in Fairy Tales," in *Evil*, edited by the Curatorium of the C. G. Jung Institute, Zurich (Evanston, Ill.: Northwestern University Press, 1967).
2. "Bei der schwartzen Frau" appeared originally in *Studien zur analytischen Psychologie C. G. Jungs II: Beiträge zur Kulturgeschichte* (Zurich, 1955), pp. 1–41. It is contained in Wilhelm Laiblin (ed.), *Märchenforschung und Tiefenpsychologie: Wege der Forschung*, vol. C II (Darmstadt: Wissenschaftliche Buchgesellschaft, 1975), pp. 299–344.
3. Marie-Louise von Franz, *Shadow and Evil in Fairy Tales* (Zurich: Spring Publications, 1974).

PART ONE

Approaches to Fairy Tales in Depth Psychology

MARIO JACOBY

C. G. Jung's View of Fairy Tale Interpretation

General Reflections on Hermeneutics in Depth Psychology

From the vantage point of depth psychology, fairy tales can be understood as depictions of psychological processes. Jung differed from Freud in evaluating creative fantasy as an autonomous phenomenon that cannot be reduced to a function of instinctual drives. There is a way to verify the interpretation of a fairy tale, namely by asking: Does the interpretation hold good for the whole course of the action rather than applying just to an individual image? Only when the presumed meaning can be followed through the entire progression of events in such a way that the sequence of motifs ultimately yields a unified meaning can we conclude that we have grasped the process and its intention.

Both of the pioneers of modern depth psychology, Sigmund Freud and C. G. Jung, brought the fairy tale into their researches at an early stage. The fairy tale arises from human fantasy, and Freud was of the opinion that "psychoanalysis is in a position to speak the decisive word in all questions that touch upon the imaginative life of man." [1] As is well known, Freud's view was that our fantasies are directed by the pleasure principle and therefore are a kind of wishful thinking. Over and against wishful thinking directed by the pleasure principle stands the reality principle, which requires adaptation to the situations of civilized life through considerable denial of instinctual drives. Culture implies restrictions, continual "reality testing." But fantasy seeks out a realm for itself in which this instinct-confining reality is suspended. This is, as Freud so aptly wrote, "an area set aside for reservation in its original state and for protection from the changes brought about by civilisation."[2] This enclave in the country of the psyche provides people with the opportunity to withdraw under certain circumstances from the demands of reality and build through fantasy their air- or pleasure-castles. In fairy tales, which in their poetic sovereignty are set above and beyond reality testing, the pleasure principle really seems to rule. We have only to consider formulations such as "In days of old, when wishing still did some good" ("The Frog King," Grimm's no. 1). Also, nearly every fairy tale has a "happy ending." Good is rewarded, evil is punished. The prince and princess find each other and "live happily ever after."

Freud recognized that myths and fairy tales can be interpreted in the way that dreams are. Thus, any interpretation must discover an array of instinctual wishes hidden behind the explicit narrative and its characters. Culture and its introjective representative in every individual, the superego, do not permit the undisguised appearance of instinctual wishes even within the nature reserve of fantasy. Thus they always appear encoded in condensed, shifted, or symbolic forms. In this way, fairy tale figures can be seen as representations of instinctual drives.

As we know, Jung saw no need to reduce human fantasy to nothing but a function of instinctual drives, even though the libido obviously plays a major role in fantasies. According to his view, fantasy representations are just as primary and primal as instincts or drives. "Man finds himself simultaneously driven to act and free to reflect."[3] Fantasy occurs spontaneously and contains nothing less than the creative potential in man. Even apart from creativity in art, which is the purest vehicle for fantasy, the development of culture would not be possible at all without the notion that the natural suchness of things can be altered. How something should be, how it could be changed, is not a question of reality but of the conceptions of human fantasy. Flying through the air, even as far as the moon—a reality today—corresponds to an age-old fantasy and longing expressed, for instance, in the myth of Daedalus and Icarus. The longing accompanying the fantasy especially contains an energic component, a human drive. Without this drive, the fantasy could never have been realized.

Fantasy is thus the fundamental element in creativity, a specifically human potentiality; therefore, in Jung's thinking, it acquires a very high value.

Let us go deeper into the nature of fantasy. It is well known that we are not the masters of our fantasies. They arise in us, they occur to us. Sometimes, in order to get fantasies and ideas, we have to reach out actively, concentrate our consciousness on fantasy possibilities, which can be quite an effort. This of course by no means guarantees that inspiration from the unconscious will come to us—creative people know this all too well. On the other side, however, it is often difficult to pry ourselves loose from our fantasies when we want to. Under some circumstances, they can be stronger than our conscious will, a fact to which certain compulsive ideas bear witness. Thus fantasizing is to a certain degree an autonomous activity that cannot be fully controlled by our ego-consciousness. As a rule, both our daydreams and our sleeping dreams are somehow bound up with our personal experience of life. For instance, young men often fantasize about women and women about men. If we investigate these fantasies, we find that they are related to the personal situation and the personal state of mind of the fantasizer. A man perhaps fantasizes about a particular woman whom he knows, fantasizes particular pleasurable or fearful situations that are somehow typical of his personal style of experience. Yet the very fact of fantasizing and dreaming about members of the opposite sex is a species-characteristic, typical activity, whatever the personal or individual coloration of the fantasy contents may be. Thus at the root of all fantasizing must lie a species-typical human potentiality that brings about and, in one way or another, organizes our fantasies, which usually appear to our conscious mind to be a function of our personal circumstances.

This ordering and regulating factor in the unconscious Jung called the archetype: "Archetypes are, by definition, factors and motifs that arrange the psychic elements into certain images, characterized as archetypal, but in such a way that they can be recognized only from the effects they produce."[4] In this connection, what Max Lüthi considers an essential characteristic of the structure of fairy tales is highly instructive: "While the novel, for example, describes lifelike characters with contradictory motivations and makeups, the fairy tale sets things out in terms of unequivocal and isolated figures. However, the visible isolation of characters and events corresponds to an all-pervasive interconnectedness, i.e., the isolated figures, through some invisible guidance, are made to fit into a harmonious interaction. The fairy tale is a story in which there are no accidents. The coordination of events is not accidental but precise. The manifest action of the tale is but the visible heights of a country that lies shrouded in mist."[5]

The invisible guiding factor in the "land of mist" can, in psychological terminology, be equated with what Jung called the archetypal background, which produces and orders psychic experience with its images and representations. This understanding clearly explains the great interest of the Jungian school in fairy-tale interpretation. In fairy tales, according to Jung, the "archetypal" regulation of human fantasy and of psychic life altogether is particularly clear. Fairy tale characters and their constellations are divested of all personal trappings; thus in them unconscious processes can be seen in their typical forms. The psychology of the unconscious can learn a great deal from fairy tales, since they describe essential human archetypal phenomena. Jung went so far as to define fairy tales as the "anatomy of the psyche."

Lüthi was right to point out that fairy tales never tell us of lifelike characters with contradictory tendencies and motivations, but rather of unitary figures who are invisibly guided into an interaction. These figures can be understood as symbol-bearers in the integral action that is presented in the fairy tale. They are not to be understood as actual people, but as symbols: they have a symbolic value in an invisibly guided process. Without them, however, the invisible guiding factor, the "archetype as such,"[6] could not be perceived. The symbols can thus be understood as sensorily perceivable tokens of the invisible ordering factor. They are the visible heights of a country shrouded in mist. Goethe once said: "True symbolism is that in which the particular represents the general, not as a dream or a shadow, but rather as a living instantaneous experience of the inpenetrable."[7] The general here would be the essentially impenetrable dimension that can be glimpsed as a living experience in a particular given image. Johann Jakob Bachofen characterized the symbol in contrast to discursive speech in the following manner: "The symbol acts on all sides of the human mind at once, whereas speech always has to address only a single thought. The symbol pushes its roots into the most secret depths of the psyche, whereas speech only touches the surface of our understanding like a light breeze. The former is directed inwards, the latter outwards. Only the symbol is capable of combining the most disparate elements into a unified total expression. Speech arranges individual elements in sequence and always only brings to consciousness piecemeal that which, to be grasped totally, would have to be presented to the mind at a single glance."[8] C. G. Jung defined the symbol as the best possible and most characteristic formulation of a relatively unknown thing.[9] Indefinable factors are unsurpassably conveyed by a living symbol. Seeing symbols, in accordance with this view, as the expression of such a dimension of depth, we touch upon the final unplumbable level of actual fairy tale interpretation. The expert on literature Wilhelm Emrich counts the folk tale among those literary works unfolding a wealth of meaning that can never be fully formulated by thought and capable of generating representative or symbolic meaning that is applicable to other life situations, periods, and outlooks. They thus comprise an "inexhaustible fabric of relationships and are susceptible of infinite reflection." [10] In other words, they have something to *say* about the mystery of being human, which can, when needed, be approximately deciphered and formulated. However, as soon as we begin to reflect about our human situation, we are caught in our own structure, since all our methods of reflection are conditioned by the nature of our consciousness. Thus we can never, so to speak, see beyond consciousness; we are stuck there, we have no Archimedean point outside of it. As Heinrich Zimmer aptly put it, "A person who discusses symbols, particularly when he is aflame with their meaning, ends up explaining his own limitations and predispositions more than exhausting the depths of the symbols." [11]

Here Zimmer calls our attention to an essential point: the meaning of a symbol does not kindle or come alive by itself. It requires the consciousness of a human person, whose own limitations and predispositions, or "personal equation," inevitably comes into play. Only when I experience it as an immediate concern can a significant meaning come alive. Yet the meaning of the symbol can never be fully exhausted, but can only be grasped within the limits of my possible understanding and the framework of the contemporary worldview to which I am attached. This being the case, we might ask if fairy tales do not become, like Rorschach tests, fields for the projection of our own fantasies once we try to understand them interpretively. We project our own ideas and conceptions on them, and in that way, the interpretation becomes more a statement about the interpreter himself than about the meaning of the tale. I believe we must acknowledge that there is no such thing as objective accuracy in fairy tale interpretation. As soon as we have the possibility of "infinite reflection," the uniqueness and limitations of the person who is reflecting become part of the picture. In this way, every interpretation has its subjective side.

Are there, however, no criteria that permit us to detect excessive subjective arbitrariness in working with fairy tales? In fact, there is a kind of evaluative sensitivity that can feel and judge whether I may be in accordance with the deepest level of the fairy tale's content. An interpretation can be an "Aha!" experience or can strike us as farfetched. Such criteria rely on our feeling for the truth, so they remain subjective. However, another very important criterion is presented by Hedwig von Beit:

> There is a control factor for verifying the accuracy of the interpretation of an image or motif, which is the complete denouement of the fairy tale. We can only assume that the essential has been grasped if an interpretation can be carried through the whole, if it can be followed not only in a single image but through the entire movement of the story, and if a unity of meaning arises out of the fullness of a long series of motifs. Just as a dream must be dealt with as a whole, just as in a painting we must consider not only individual figures but all of them in relationship to one another and as intentional means of expression on the part of the artist, in the same way it is necessary to investigate the fairy tale as a whole, taking all of its characters into account. We cannot limit our interest to the movement of the main characters any more than we could with a play, for single threads do not constitute a fabric. For each of the motifs in a fairy tale has a very definite and inalienable place in the structure; this is so much the case that even the same motifs appearing in different places in the action have to be interpreted differently. A purely external compilation of like motifs is a preliminary labor following which the special function of the

image in a given fairy tale still has to be looked into. Only in terms of the interconnectedness of all the figures in the fairy tale does the homogeneous meaning of the action arise. Only in this overall context can the closed circle of images be surveyed and interpreted.[12]

As a means of objective verification, this criterion is of crucial importance.

Hedwig von Beit mentions the compilation of like motifs as preliminary work in the interpretation of fairy tales. Here she is referring to a method that Jung called *amplification*. Whenever nothing meaningful occurs to us with regard to a particular motif, it is a good idea to research where in the history of symbols the same or a similar motif or figure crops up. For example, in most fairy tales some animal appears. In order to get an idea of the meaning of this animal, it is helpful to make a compilation of conceptions that have been projected on it. Let us say, for example, that we have a raven. It is a bird; its element is the air. In contrast to humans, birds, by their nature, can fly and thus might possibly represent flights of thought. The air element is after all associated with the mental and fantastic, with the immaterial. That is why we call wishful fantasies "castles in the air." Colloquially, we say someone is "cuckoo" if they tend to be absorbed in strange thoughts or fantasies. The raven is a black bird. According to a Greek myth, the raven was originally white, but since it brought Apollo the bad news of the death of his beloved, out of anger and sadness Apollo transformed it into a black bird. As the bearer of bad news, the raven is associated with bad luck or misfortune. It is connected with black thoughts and fantasies and with a fearful or depressive mood.

Amplification, as can be seen from this example, is a method for probing the meaning of a symbol. Perhaps in the case of the raven we might have come to the same conclusion without amplification just by concentrating on how a raven strikes our mood and feeling. Letting oneself be struck directly in this manner by an impression of the figure in question is, in my opinion, at least as important as amplification. Amplification can then serve to verify whether or not our personal reaction jibes with general conceptions. In addition, in cases where, with particular figures and motifs, we have no reaction of our own and nothing occurs to us, amplification can help us directly.[13]

In looking for the homogeneous meaning of a fairy tale, weight should be placed on its particular typical structure. For example, quite a few fairy tales begin with a king encountering a crisis: his wife has died, his hunters are getting lost in the forest, he has no children, is old and sick, has run out of the elixir of life, and so on. It could also be that he is hardhearted. The tale then usually describes how this crisis is resolved. Either the king is reestablished in some new way or he is replaced by the prince or by fortune's favored young man. However, many deeds and events in the realm of magic lie on the way to this renewal.

What is the meaning of the symbol of the king in fairy tales? Amplication tells us the following: kingship is an age-old institution that we find among many archaic tribes. For instance, in Egypt, the pharaoh was considered the direct scion of the sun god Amon-Ra or of Horus. He was thus an embodiment of the divine on earth and therefore possessed unrestricted power. Louis XIV, the "Sun King," made the famous statement, "L'état, c'est moi." There is a well-grounded suspicion extant that in his old age Charles de Gaulle, "le grand président du soleil" (the great sun president), was overcome and inflated by the archetype of divine kingship. Thus the king originally represented an embodiment of divine power and knowledge; he was descended from the luminosity par excellence, from the sun, the symbol of consciousness. The king, in issuing his laws and commands, was thus illuminated by divine consciousness. We find a similar idea in the dogma of the infallibility of the pope when he is speaking ex cathedra. His words are then considered to be inspired by the Holy Ghost. It is noteworthy that in many archaic cultures, although the king possessed unrestricted divine power, this was the case only so long as everything was going well for the tribe. In the case of plague, defeat in war, or other similar misfortune, the king was considered to have lost his *mana*. He had lost his divine force, and someone else had to become king. In this way, the king symbol is superpersonal.

We find this motif in the myth of King Oedipus, whose kingship was called into question by the outbreak of plague among his people. The Old Testament recounts something similar in the story of Saul and David. In the middle of Saul's reign, the divine kingship was conferred upon David by the seer Samuel. "The spirit of the Lord" had turned away from Saul, and he was tormented by an evil spirit. He yielded ever more to depression, degenerated into a cruel tyrant, and finally fell in battle. Even modern political leaders sometimes have "charisma" attributed to them. But then even the slightest lapse (as happened, for example, in the case of Henry Kissinger) immediately means the leader loses "a point from his crown."

From the inner psychic point of view, the king symbolizes human consciousness as the creator and spokesman of the categories of order and value. It is the symbol of an inner norm, a "God-given" exemplary image, and therefore has something sacrosanct about it; it is a pervasively binding guideline. As a dominant factor in the collective consciousness, it symbolizes the existing code of values, whether written or not. To a great extent it is the "one" principle, in the sense that "one" does this but "one" does not do that. In general, this "one" exercises greater dominance over us than we realize. We require general norms and a consensus of outlook as guidelines in dealing with ourselves and the demands of society. The symbol of the king is inherent in the human psychic makeup and to a great degree corresponds to the psychological component that Freudian metapsychology calls the superego. Thus when many fairy tales begin with a crisis in the kingship and go on to describe its renewal, they are expressing a profound truth. It is natural and inevitable for new living ideas, new creations of a religious, ideological, or political nature, to lose their immediate potency once they have been established and have acquired followers and an organization. One one hand, the king stands for the creative consciousness principle: cultural development is an enormous creative achievement for humanity. However, once the creative principle is institutionalized and organized for use, it is unavoidably exposed to an obsolescence and a rigidity that increasingly oppose it to life: the elixir of life has been lost. Now new, potentially dominant values manifest that compensate for the old in terms of the complexity and vigor of the human psyche. The prince or new hero can be understood as the bearer of these new possibilities. This is an example of how we can find a basic meaning in the variety of fairy tales that are concerned with the renewal of the king. Psychic renewal and transformation is portrayed in such a process together with all its inherent enormous difficulties and conflicts. The indispensable "golden hair," for example, complete with certain crucial knowledge, must be gotten from the devil under great peril in a sooty cave, or a treacherous and powerful dragon must be vanquished.

Since fairy tales are abstract and, to a certain extent, timeless, nothing is expressed in them about the content of the current prevailing worldview. The content also changes, but the structure remains, whether we are talking about collective historic upheavals or the transformational process of the individual human being. Practically, in getting at the possible meanings of a fairy tale, it is sometimes helpful to ask ourselves what a motif constellation might mean if it came up in a dream. All the figures in the fairy tale would then be understood as the psychic potencies and personal tendencies of the dreamer him- or herself and the hero or heroine as closest to the ego. Working with a dream, we would then relate the entire action to the conscious situation of the dreamer. The personality of the dreamer would be our reference point. However, there is no such reference point in a fairy tale, for it is related to the human situation in general and, seen psychologically, portrays collective psychic processes. Thus for an interpretation to have living relevance, it seems to me important to look for practical examples of how an archetypal constellation in a fairy tale could transpire in the here and now. In doing this, we make a connection between the timeless, general, typical human situation and the current flow of personal experience. The archetypal comes alive when its meaning is realized in terms of individual experience. When a fairy tale tells us, for example, that the knowledge of the cause of a spring's drying up or of the barrenness of an apple tree must be sought from the devil,[14] we may be reminded of certain therapeutic experiences in depth psychology. Dealing with the "bedeviled" part of oneself, that which has been repressed and condemned, is conducive to consciousness expansion and maturation, and may lead in an experiential fashion to the liberation of blocked energies. This is only a minor example of how fairy tales express psychological knowledge in a symbolic way.

In sum, we could say that fairy tales can be understood from the psychological point of view as the self-portrayal of psychic processes. Therefore they are eminently interesting for the psychology of the unconscious. C. G. Jung wrote: "In myths and fairytales, as in dreams, the psyche tells its own story, and the interplay of the archetypes is revealed in its natural setting as 'formation, transformation/the eternal Mind's eternal recreation.'"[15]

NOTES

1. Sigmund Freud, *The Standard Edition of the Complete Psychological Works of Sigmund Freud*, edited and translated by James Strachey (London: Hogarth, 1957), vol. 19, p. 208.
2. Freud, *Standard Edition*, vol. 8, p. 235.
3. C. G. Jung, *Collected Works*, vol. 8 (Princeton, N.J.: Princeton University Press), para. 406.

4. Jung, *CW* 11, para. 222.

5. Max Lüthi, *Das europäische Volksmärchen* (Bern: Franke, 1960).

6. See Jung, *CW* 8, para. 417.

7. Johann Wolfgang von Goethe, "Maximen und Reflexionen," in *Schriften der Goethe-Gesellschaft*, vol. 21 (1907), p. 314.

8. Johann Jakob Bachofen, *Mutterrecht und Urreligion* (Leipzig, 1927), pp. 6off.

9. See Jung, *CW* 6, para. 815.

10. Wilhelm Emrich, "Wertung und Rangordnung literarischer Werke," in *Sprache in Technischen Zeitalter*, vols. 11–12 (1964), pp. 9off.

11. Cited in Hedwig von Beit, *Symbolik des Märchens* (Bern: Franke, 1960), p. 15.

12. Ibid., pp. 15–16.

13. A treasure trove of general ideas related to a given motif is H. Bachtold-Stäubli (ed.), *Handwörterbuch des deutschen Aberglaubens* (Berlin and Leipzig: W. de Gruyter, 1927).

14. "The Devil with the Three Golden Hairs" (Grimm's no. 29).

15. Jung, *CW* 9, 1, para. 400.

VERENA KAST

How Fairy Tales Deal with Evil

Thematic Approaches to the Fairy Tale as a Dynamic Process

We can approach fairy tales with many different kinds of questions, and it is fascinating to observe the new perspectives and processes of psychic being that continually emerge. One possibility, for instance, is to look at fairy tales from the thematic standpoint of the confrontation between good and evil. That is quite a workable way of looking at them. However, the conclusion that is generally drawn—that good always triumphs over evil in fairy tales—should perhaps be reconsidered. The most prevalent fairy tale pattern gives evil a special function in the psychic transformation process depicted by the narrative. But there is also a second pattern in which evil cannot be transformed. Fairy tales show, through subtly diversified processes, how *and* when *one can deal with which evils.*

The first thing that strikes us in investigating the question of evil is that fairy tales always show us that evil is not simply evil. Most characters can be both good and evil at the same time. For instance, wolves devour baby goats and grandmothers, but they can also be helpful. One fairy tale recounts how, when a wolf was spared being shot, it gave up one of its hairs; when the hero would twist the hair, the wolf would come to his aid. There is also the case of the two hunters in "The Two Brothers" (Grimm's no. 60), who, though they were hungry, refrained from killing a wolf because it begged for its life; they were then given two cubs who later helped them to defeat a dragon. Some of us will remember the little couplet: "Hunter, hunter let me live, / To you two young cubs I'll give."

Things also can be good or evil. The forest, for example, often appears as the tortuous wood that we cannot find our way out of. But the forest can also have a protective or nurturing function.

Princesses are not only very beautiful, sweet, and angelic; they can also be quite evil. They can, for example, kill all their suitors, either actively or passively. The riddle-posing princess who kills every suitor who cannot solve her riddle does it actively. It is done passively, for example, by Sleeping Beauty, who in her innocent slumber lures many a prince to rescue her before the time is ripe. They are left hanging in the briers.

Even the good and beautiful Snow White (Grimm's no. 53) is repeatedly disobedient. In a Swiss version of the story, the dwarves even hold a vote for this reason to decide whether or not to fry her up in a pan. Princes forget their brides on the outskirts of town and do not follow the advice they have been given; they even sometimes try to kill children. Kings can also be evil. For example, in "The Devil with the Three Golden Hairs" (Grimm's no. 29), the king tries by all available means to get rid of the fortune-favored lad who is to receive his daughter's hand in marriage.

It is the other way around with witches, whom many people regard as fundamentally evil. The Russian Baba Yaga, for example, can help the hero find his princess. Whether she devours or is helpful is frequently a matter of what tone one chooses in addressing her. A good example is Ivan's way of dealing with Baba Yaga in "The Virgin Czarina." After various struggles, Ivan wins through to the road of death, where he comes to the hut of Baba Yaga. Following custom, he knocks on the cross and then bows.

Baba Yaga then appears and asks him: "How is it, my little one? Are you riding with or against your will?" Then the bold youth leaps at the old woman and cries:

> Now I'm going to box your ear,
> I'll make an ovenhole of your rear.
> I'll crush the scab up with my hand
> Till out of your bum comes pouring sand!

> Old woman, you should know better than to ask a hero all those questions. First you should supply food and drink!

The witch is now at his service. She gives him food and a horse as well, and provides him with safe conduct. She also reveals where he will find the Virgin Czarina, the beautiful Maria.

What is interesting here is Ivan's way of dealing with Baba Yaga, this mother-witch figure. Calling him "my little one," she really intends to render him impotent and devour him. He puts up a forceful defense. His rhymed speech, which sounds like an incantation, seems to work quite well. Through it he reassures himself of his strength, and does not allow himself to be rendered impotent.

However, we must not forget that there are some demonic powers that almost never turn out to be good. I know of no positive Bluebeard, for instance, and giants are almost never good, nor are giantesses. Master warlocks, demonic sorcerers, are figures that seem to take pleasure in being evil.

What is evil?

To begin with, let us call evil that which opposes and obstructs the fairy tale hero and his will, or which disrupts his preexisting situation. This would of course leave room for the hero himself to be evil, for example, by violating prohibitions. This indeed he continually does and must do, since otherwise change is not possible. For this reason, we should not regard evil as a known quantity. By understanding evil as that which obstructs, various levels and qualities of evil emerge.

There is no question about the presence of evil in fairy tales. Now, if we want to clarify the function of evil, it might be helpful to ask ourselves what the most common structure for fairy tales is. Let us call this most common fairy tale structure the first structure to distinguish it from a second, specialized structure. The starting point for most fairy tales is a situation of deficiency. The fruit of a special tree is stolen, there is no princess in the land, or the queen is unable to have children. These situations of deficiency betoken through images that there is evil afoot. The exact nature of this evil emerges in the course of the story. The conclusion of the tale usually shows quite clearly what the deficiency actually was. However, it is only rarely the case that at the end of the narrative the original situation is simply restored, perhaps completed by the presence of a missing person; rather, a new level is attained, a development is accomplished. The prince never just gets a new princess, leaving the old one to her own devices; in the process of seeking the princess, he himself changes; he is always on the move, in flux. Externally this development is expressed by the prince's finally becoming king. Such a successful conclusion harbors more possibilities, more liberties than were present at the outset. The initial situation could be compared to a neurotic condition characterized by an extremely limited set of possibilities. The end is then like a post-neurotic condition in which the patient has abandoned various compulsive ruts and can once again take advantage of his opportunities. A collective situation can also be neurotic. There is no great distinction between a totalitarian system and a collective neurosis. Fairy tales can compensate for collective neuroses. The way that leads from the initial events of the fairy tale, which depict the situation of deficiency, to its rectification on another level of development can only go by way of a confrontation with evil. Evil manifests itself as soon as a process of development stagnates. It thus provides a spur for further evolution, confrontation, and the realization of all our strengths. At this point, the hero either prevails or else fails to be a hero in the fairy tale sense.

There is also a second structure to be found in fairy tales that is much less common than the one I have just described. Again, it begins with a situation of deficiency, and again there is a confrontation with obstructing powers. However, in the case of the second structure, this does not lead to a process of development and maturation; rather, all means must be engaged in order to escape a nasty situation. The heroes and heroines are happy just to be able to save their own skin. I think of particular versions of the Bluebeard story, for example, "L'Ours à la holte." Bluebeard is a man of great riches. He tries to court a girl. She resists at first, because Bluebeard has a blue beard and is outlandish. Then, out of consideration for his wealth, she gives in. She goes to live in Bluebeard's castle. Bluebeard tells her that he has to take a journey. He gives her the keys but forbids her to enter a particular chamber. Nevertheless, she enters and finds pieces of female corpses hanging and tubs of blood standing around. Out of fright, she drops the key, which becomes spotted with blood. No matter how hard she scrubs, the blood will not come out. At this moment, Bluebeard comes back and kills her as well. Then he goes and brings back her sister on the pretext that she should help his wife to pass the time. The same thing happens, and then he goes to fetch the other sister, the youngest one. She is less timid and less naive than her older sisters. She just looks into the room and leaves the key sticking in the door. Now Bluebeard decides to marry this sister, because in his opinion, she has passed the test. She agrees, but demands of him that he must first bring some laundry all the way to her parents without ever putting the basket down. Bluebeard agrees to do so. In the meantime, the girl brings her sisters back to life, puts them in a basket, climbs in herself, and Bluebeard carries them home. Whenever he wants to pause to take a rest, the third sister calls from the basket that she sees him, and he should keep going. Thus at the end the three sisters are home again, and Bluebeard is once more alone in his castle.

There are other versions of the story in which Bluebeard is at least killed by the sister's brothers. In the version I have just recounted, however, though lives have been saved, nothing new has been gained. No development has taken place. In this second structural form, we are definitely dealing with a different kind of evil than in the first, though the boundaries between the two are blurred. Further examples of the second structural form would be fairy tales in which the protagonist is killed. For example, in "Frau Trude," a girl approaches Frau Trude in a disrespectful way, and Frau Trude turns her into a block of wood and throws her into the fire. I also count as having the second structure those tales in which the hero does not fulfill his task. Such fairy tales are still relatively common in old collections. As an example, I might cite "The Fiery Lizard."[1]

> Once a tailor came to Andreasberg, but not quite all the way. No, he came as far as Hollenwife Place and remained there. It was such a lovely evening, not really dark but not light either, just a lovely summer evening in the Harz Mountains. He thought: "Why not just lie down here. Spare yourself the price of an inn. After all, there are no wild animals around here."
>
> In a trice, moss was gathered, a bed was made, and the tailor was upon it. In a few minutes he had no business with the world. He was sleeping like a log, when all of a sudden it was as though someone had jerked his eyes open. The mountain was red like the sky at sunset, but he couldn't see any flames or anything else that would make the mountain so red. As he looked on in astonishment, he saw that the redness was coming from lower down on the mountain and climbing higher and higher. He saw in fact that a large dangerous lizard was creeping up the mountain and casting the

red color upon it. He wanted to leap up, but he couldn't. It was as though he was fastened to the spot. The monstrous creature was coming slowly in his direction, closer and closer. Of course our tailor became not a little frightened— anyhow, tailors are not a stouthearted breed. But no matter what he did, he couldn't move from the spot. The cold sweat of fear stood out on his body.

The creature was glowing all over, and its fanged maw was agape. He could even see its hot breath and its eyes glared right at him. "Whoa," he thought, "that thing wants your blood, it'll do you in for sure!" It was still about twenty paces away when the clock in the Glockenberg Tower struck twelve. With the last toll of the bell, everything disappeared, and darkness covered the mountain. Here and there, the stars peeked through the clouds, and beyond, from the place where morning comes from, the moon rose. The tailor was also able to stand up, and straight into Andreasberg he went. There he met the watchman who was sounding midnight. The tailor asked him if he could give him a place for the night. The tailor was brought to the nightwatchman's quarters and there he stayed until morning. But not a word did he say about what had happened to him.

In the morning, round about ten o'clock, he went to the pastor and told him about the incident on the Hollenwife Place. The pastor said that he meant to accompany him there that evening, and they would see what would happen then. The tailor shouldn't be afraid. The lizard was surely under a curse, and the tailor had to release it. But to do that he would have to be brave and also he mustn't talk, otherwise everything would be spoiled. All right, said the tailor, he would gather all his courage; nonetheless, the lizard was a hideous monster. Even though that was the case, the pastor said, he would still have to kiss it.

That evening at half past ten, they went together to the place, sat down together on the ground, and the pastor spoke again to the tailor: As I read in this book now, you be completely still and let come whatever comes, even if the lizard half kills you. You'll see, it will be to your good fortune and mine, and to the lizard's good fortune too. We'll all be rich. There's definitely something behind this. The tailor promised to follow this advice.

They waited until eleven struck. When the hour struck, the mountain gradually became brighter and brighter, this time far brighter than the time before. They could already see the lizard slowly creeping up the mountainside. This time it was far more fiery and more hideous, and was also approaching faster. The pastor read what he could and tried to encourage the tailor. He gave him frequent comforting looks and signaled him to keep his courage up. At last the lizard came so near that its glowing paws were on the tailor's leg. He felt its hot, venomous breath coming out between its fiery fangs. It climbed higher up on him. His heart beat fast. The pastor read and looked at him sharply, as if to say: "Hold out, don't give up."

At the end the lizard was nearly up to his mouth. Its breath, reeking of sulphur, soon took his own breath away. It wanted to kiss him, but then he could hold out no longer. Revolted, he turned his face away, and at that moment, the clock struck twelve. With the first toll of the bell, everything disappeared. Chagrined and angry, the pastor said: No, another such fool, another such lilyliver as the tailor was nowhere to be found. If he had only held out another instant, it would have turned the trick. But the tailor said: If he hadn't turned away at that moment, he would have suffocated.

So it was all in vain, and they went back home together. On the following evening at the same time they returned. Everything happened just as before. But this time the mountain glowed so brightly, it was like daylight, and the lizard gave out flames from its entire body. The tailor resolved to do better this time. He held out until the lizard was nearly touching him with its fangs, but then his courage deserted him and again he turned his face away. At that moment the clock struck twelve, and everything disappeared. Then in the distance they heard a wailing and a screaming, as though a young girl were crying very hard. Then the pastor said: "It's all over with. Our fear and effort has been in vain. The creature must now remain accursed."

From that time on, no more has been seen of it, and the mountain has never turned red again, except in the evening sunset. Then indeed the mountain again takes on something of a red appearance. The tailor continued his travels, but he told the keeper of the inn where he stayed the next day what had happened in Andreasberg, and it was the innkeeper who passed the story along.

Regarding stories with the first structural form, it is possible to ask if the evil involved is really evil. Or we could phrase the question the other way around: Isn't what we experience as evil something that demands change or some development from us, or challenges us to confrontation? But that would only illustrate the difficulties involved in changing oneself. After all, every change to some extent involves death and rebirth. This is often symbolized in fairy tales by the hero being killed and brought back to life.

In the case of the second structure, we can speak of real evil. Here "evil" would mean that a destructive power was at work that could not be dealt with, only avoided. Flight is the only possibility here, even at the price of the hero or heroine returning ostensibly untransformed. Our heroine in the Bluebeard story at least knows that she ought not to go back to Bluebeard's castle. This could be understood as meaning that she can no longer permit the expression of her destructive side, or her pleasure in the destructive element, even in the smallest ways. Otherwise she will end up back in Bluebeard's clutches, seized by a blind and uncontrollable destructiveness.

The question is, how we should deal with each kind of evil?

Fairy tales show us the answer to this question in a very nuanced fashion.

There is a parallel here to typical human patterns of behavior. One response to evil is to respect its dark power. This pattern is a prerequisite for dealing with evil. Respect expresses a justified fear of evil. We acknowledge our fear, yet we relate with this darkness. We accept it, and thus we also take it with us. An example of this is the story of "The Two Brothers" (Grimm's no. 60). The wild animals in this story are not to be killed, but rather taken along. Wild animals can be symbols for various wild, unarticulated, undomesticated drives in us—various shadings of our aggressive behavior, which we tend to view as "bad." However, when the animals are taken along, to return to the fairy tale image, they are very helpful. They only become evil if we try to kill them, that is, if we try to suppress the aggressive energy that they represent.

Loving acceptance is one way of taking this energy on; wrathful acceptance is another. Both are emotional ways of coping. "The Frog King" (Grimm's no. 1) comes to mind. In that case, we can hardly speak of loving acceptance. Nonetheless, the princess takes the frog in her hand before she dashes him against the wall, at which point he turns into a prince. In the fairy tale "The Princess in the Tree," the hero has to bring twelve lambs with him to feed the wolves, otherwise they will rip his horse to shreds. This is also a form of acceptance, an acceptance of the need to feed our wolves, to nourish our wolfish side.

In the fairy tale "The Lilting, Leaping Lark" (Grimm's no. 88), the father must abandon his youngest daughter to a lion, because, in order to fulfull a wish of this same daughter, he has penetrated in an unallowable fashion into the territory of the lion. The father is inconsolable, but the youngest daughter says, "A promise must be kept. I will surely be able to soothe the lion." However, she has no need to soothe him, for at night he is a wonderful handsome prince and a lion by day only.

Here we see how the fairy tale is prepared to accept this lion-like element, trusting that it is not so evil as all that. And that is the first step toward redeeming the lion. A parallel version, "The Summer Garden and the Winter Garden,"[2] tells not of a lion but of a dragonlike monster. At one point, the girl returns home, and the monster asks her not to stay away too long. But she stays away for a long time. When she comes back, the monster is gone. Finally, after a long search, she finds it in a garden lying under some leaves, seemingly lifeless. The girl throws herself down and kisses this monster—and a wonderful handsome prince appears before her. Loving acceptance can also have the effect of liberating this apparent evil from its spell. However, the girl is always liberated at the same time.

We find a very fine form of this acceptance in a Hungarian fairy tale.[3] There the hero addresses the iron-toothed witch as "Lady Mother." To this she replies: "It's fortunate that you called me mother, otherwise your bones would soon have been smaller than poppy seeds." The hero sees what is happening, namely, that he might get crushed. This shows that he is not ignorant of evil. Yet he reminds the witch that, in spite of everything, she could also be a "mother"; he reminds her of and addresses her good side. This is a tactic that we often use: we invoke the good side of people, not their destructive side. This is also something we can do with regard to ourselves. For example, if I discover about myself that I have a side that is so voracious that it would gladly devour everything, I can try giving something up rather than simply consuming. And if I am lucky, this brings about a change.

Knowing about the destructive side but nevertheless addressing the kernel of good is similar to the act of denial in fairy tales. I am referring here to those tales in which, for example, one opens a forbidden chamber, say the hundredth one, to which of course one has been given the key. Later one denies that one has been inside. I am particularly reminded here of tales of the type of "Mary's Child" (Grimm's no. 3), but prefer to stick to the pre-

Christian version, "The Black Woman."[4] In the revised Christian versions, the matter becomes very complicated, because of course in those versions the Christian image of woman has to be brought into the picture.

A poor farmer who has run out of money places his daughter in the service of a black woman, for which he receives a great deal of money. He is relieved of his cares without having done anything for it. The girl cleans the black woman's palace, and when the three years are nearly up, she opens up the hundredth chamber, which has been forbidden her. There she sees the black woman, who has become almost white. In response to the black woman's question whether she has been in the chamber, she denies that she has. Then she is banished to the forest.

There a king's son finds the girl and marries her. The young queen brings children into the world; the black woman appears and asks if she has been in the hundredth chamber. The queen denies it; the black woman takes one of the children away and makes the queen deaf. The mother-in-law speaks of her daughter-in-law as a child murderer. This happens three times. The second time the black woman makes the queen dumb, the third time blind.

Then the queen is to be burned as a witch. At this moment, the black woman comes, brings the three children, and asks one last time if the queen has been in the forbidden chamber. Once again the queen denies that she has. At that point the black woman becomes white, gives the queen the three children, and sends her back to the castle. She says: "If you had once said you had been inside, I would have reduced you to dust and ashes." Then, to top matters off, the evil mother-in-law ends up being burned at the stake.

What possibilities were open to this girl? She need not have opened the door to the hundredth chamber, that is, she need not have yielded to the impulse toward disobedience, which really came from the black woman who was herself in need of redemption. (The black woman represents an unconscious content that needs to be liberated, in other words, needs to be included in conscious life.) Then the girl would have been sent home again and maybe, even quite surely, richly rewarded. Maybe the black woman would have turned white, but the girl herself would have undergone little transformation. She could also have opened the door and then admitted it, in which case, according to the declaration of the black woman, she would have been reduced to dust and ashes. This would have been the most dangerous solution. Being reduced to dust and ashes surely means that the entire ego-personality would have been shattered. Honesty here would not have paid off. The girl chose the third possible solution: She opened the door, looked inside, then steadfastly denied it. For that, her children were taken from her and she was portrayed as a child murderer. However, her consistent denial, even at the stake, ultimately led to success. The black woman turned white and the evil mother-in-law died. A major mother problem is worked through here. The dark mother disappears; the girl can now be a mother herself. Her transformation is complete.

Lots of "evil" takes place in this fairy tale, from the very beginning. The father is at his wits' end—here is the condition of need that should spur him to some undertaking. But instead he sells his daughter and makes a tidy sum on the deal. Fathers who sacrifice their children, frequently even before they are born, often appear at the beginning of fairy tales. In the course of such tales, the child must confront the demonic forces, usually as an adult. For example, this takes place in the tale "The Girl without Hands" (Grimm's no. 31) or "The King's Son and the Devil's Daughter."[5] This motif of sacrificing a child could mean sacrificing freshly awakened energies to a state of depression: "After all, there is no way out. . . ." But that is too facile an abandonment of hope for development, and it is a betrayal of the unconscious.

Moreover, such fathers are, in fairy tales, never transformed. It almost seems that the older generation must die untransformed.

The challenge to disobedience in our tale comes from the "black woman." She forbids opening the hundredth chamber, and the girl obeys for almost three years. Then her curiosity is aroused against this prohibition, and she disobeys.

All the same, the girl cleaned the rooms in the black woman's palace for nearly three years, and obviously at the same time she also cleansed the dark mother herself. So she has lived many different aspects of the dark side of her psyche, experienced them and worked on them. Her disobedience results in the girl seeing the black woman and almost liberating her. But it also brings about her separation from the black woman. These two things actually belong together: separation through seeing and knowledge, and separation as a step toward liberation.

Denial in this case means wanting not to have been seen by this aspect of the psyche, by this unwholesome but also definitely fascinating side of herself, and also, especially, not wanting to have been in it, in the same room with this black woman. Denial creates distance from this psychic content, this split-off darkness, and it shows that the girl knows the danger of this side of herself. She avoids being identified with this darkness, and she avoids as well the inflation that is possible when one associates with the power of evil. The consequences of this denial are, to begin with, banishment to the forest, then loss of speech, hearing, and sight—loss of communication in the broadest sense. One can tell the world nothing of what is happening within. The further consequence is the worst: loss of the children. The black woman steals the children because she needs them.

From the psychological point of view, this means that all energies are directed inward rather than outward. We have here an uncompromising state of introversion, and what is going on within it cannot be articulated. But this is exactly what brings about the transformation. Consciousness expresses denial and suffers to the utmost—in silence; and through this tremendous encapsulation, the destructive complex is transformed.

With the first child stolen, the girl becomes deaf; with the second, dumb; with the third, blind. This extreme degree of forced introversion is demanded in order to preserve the self, not least because, with the evil mother-in-law nearby, the girl might have gotten seriously entangled with the dark feminine principle.

This tale exhibits a very nuanced attitude toward "the dark one," as the black woman can surely be called. To begin with we have the girl working in the black woman's house, which suggests she is working with darkness—her own darkness as well as a transpersonal darkness. Then there is her experience of having seen this darkness and yet not having seen it, which is really a respectful acceptance and rejection at the same time. The rejection is her desperate attempt to distance herself from this overwhelmingly powerful darkness, which is bound up with tremendous suffering. But the heroine's disobedience is absolutely necesary; it paves the way for the definitive separation from the "dark mother."

A way of dealing with evil other than denial is combat, of which the most common form is the motif of combat with a dragon. Talking nicely to a dragon is of little help. An active decision must be taken. Combat as an active form of confrontation with evil occurs primarily in tales like "The Two Brothers" (Grimm's no. 60). The two brothers, sons of a poor man, have eaten the heart and liver of a golden bird; as a result, each morning they find a golden egg under their pillows. After completing their apprenticeship with a hunter, they go forth into the world, and one of the brothers frees a town from a dragon which until then had taken one of its virgins every year. He is able to overcome this dragon with the help of his animals and thus wins the hand of the king's daughter.

The dragon menaces the world of consciousness. It demands unreasonable sacrifices—every year a virgin—and this sacrifice of virgins will sooner or later undermine life as a whole. We know that many knights have already been killed by this dragon, but our hunter is able to kill it. So when must one flee from this menacing monster? When *can* one kill the dragon? The matter seems to depend on the hero's stage of development when encountering the dragon. In this dragon-killer tale, the two brothers have already completed their apprenticeship with the hunter. They already have their forest lore and they already have their animals—from hares to lions. They find a golden egg under their pillows each morning and, to top it off, there are two of them. Thus we can say that they already have experience in dealing with the unconscious. The dragon, the devourer, the menace, is constellated at a time when the brothers are already quite well equipped for a fight.

The dragon can be interpreted psychologically as an old undifferentiated side of the psyche that wants again to swallow up what consciousness has already worked through. Killing the dragon might betoken stilling the voice in oneself that tries to persuade one after the completion of a major task that nothing has been accomplished, that everything is as it was before. In that way, the whole accomplishment is swallowed up again.

But in fairy tales, one combats evil more often with trickery than with force.

In "Hansel and Gretel" (Grimm's no. 15) the witch was destroyed through Gretel's pretense that she had no idea how to get into the oven as the witch commanded. The impatient witch illustrates it by doing it herself. Gretel only has to give her one last push and close the oven door. Thus Gretel appropriates the witch's intentions and uses them against her—in that way, she annihilates her. This of course presupposes that Gretel also has witchlike qualities, otherwise she never would have been able to guess what the witch intended. We find a trick with a similar effect in "Thumbling" (in Perrault, "Petit Poucet"). Having ended up in the clutches of a man-eating monster, at night Thumbling puts the little gold crowns of the man-eater's daughters on himself and his brothers, and the boys' black hats on the daughters. The man-eater then kills his daughters, who have already developed quite bloodthirsty tendencies. Here again it is a case of foreseeing what the man-eater would do. One has to outsmart him and have a good imagination for evil. That is another form of acceptance of evil. This is especially valuable in relationships: in this way one is better attuned to one's partner and is ultimately less likely to be disappointed.

Trickery also works against giants. Take, for example, the "brave little tailor" who throws stones from a tree at the chests of the two giants below—with the result that they become enraged at each other and beat each other to death. Besides having to be clever enough to use trickery, the little tailor also had to guess that the giants would be stupid enough to react that way.

Giants are gigantically stupid, large, violent, angry, and raging. They can stand for our very unstructured affects (giant fear, giant anger). The little tailor's example is counsel to remain *above* these affects, that is, sit in the tree above. In that way, he is able to watch them as their behavior unfolds and he can simply let them play themselves out. Giant affects are affects that are stronger than conscious control—they do not belong in the community.

One can also deal with the devil through trickery. In the Grimm's fairy tale "The Farmer and the Devil" (no. 189), one night the farmer sees a fire in his field with a black devil dancing in it. "Are you sitting on a treasure?" the little farmer asks. The devil is glad to give him the treasure, because he has money enough; it is the fruits of the earth that he longs for. Thus he gives the farmer the money on the condition that for two years he receives half the harvest from the field. As a means of avoiding dispute, the farmer proposes to give what grows above the earth the first year and what grows under the earth the second year. The first year, he plants turnips, and thus the devil ends up with only withered leaves. The second year he plants wheat. The devil disappears in a rage down a cleft in the rock, and the farmer gets the treasure.

The farmer drives the devil away from the treasure, but does not liberate him. To me it seems that the devil has a certain longing for deliverance because he craves the fruits of the earth; in other words, he wants to get involved with the human world. Each time has its own individual sense of what is devilish or diabolical. The devil is not simply a fixed quantity. In addition, each one of us individually considers different things diabolical. We may conclude that the devil is a name for that which is driven furthest from our consciousness. In view of all this, one might almost feel sorry that no deliverance is possible for the devil here.

If, however, we assume that the side of the psyche embodied by the devil is too dangerous to be lived and experienced, then the farmer's behavior is correct. He sees a shadow problem but does not feed it; rather, in a humorous fashion he cultivates the side of the psyche to which the devil cannot gain access. In this way he acquires the treasure in the form of money, in other words, in the form of energy connected with that side.

The main gist of this tale is that evil is not impossible to overcome, but one has to observe precisely and then employ the strategy of cultivating in an area where the devil has no power. So often we want to undertake something precisely in an area where the devil does have power. Generally speaking, the use of trickery or strategy presupposes a familiarity with the person one wants to outwit and the ability to predict his behavior. But this means that one has to have quite good insight into such figures of evil, and we are not born with such insight. One has to have acquired insight into one's own shadow side, into one's own evil, so that one is no longer experiencing, knowing, and combating evil purely as a projection.

If neither force nor trickery is effective, then there is *flight*, which often involves elements of trickery. We see a good example of magical flight in the Grimm's fairy tale "The Water Nixie" (no. 79):

Two children, a brother and sister, are playing near a well. They fall in and are taken prisoner by a water nixie. At one point while she is in church, the two children take flight. Of course the water nixie is quick to see what has happened and goes after them. The little girl throws down a brush behind them, which grows into a brush mountain that the nixie has to climb over. Then the little boy throws a comb down beside him, which grows into a comb mountain that the nixie has to climb over. Then the little girl throws down a mirror behind her, and that grows into a mirror mountain, forcing the nixie to go back home and get an axe to cut the mountain in two. By this time, the two children have gotten away, and the nixie has to take herself off back to her well.

In other magical-flight tales—for example, in the Russian story "The Girl as a Soldier"—instead of the mirror, there is a pebble that turns into a river. Baba Yaga guzzles herself to death by drinking the river up and finally exploding.

Magical flight is always flight from a witch, an evil sorcerer, or the devil himself. One flees from an elementary menace for the sake of survival. One flees and throws things back, making offerings of what the pursuer wants, what belongs to him, and thus what binds one to him—for when nothing more binds one to the pursuer, then he can find no point to attack. For women, these offerings are mostly objects that are connected with feminine vanity. Men, on the other hand, offer saddlebags or riding crops.[6] Here, one is giving up one's own urge for power. One is saved by becoming completely simple, giving up all possessions, even down to the last little pebble. When one gives up all claims to power, then that grasping, greedy side of the psyche that is behind such claims comes to a halt. If it appears again after a certain period of time—unconscious constellations do indeed seem to have a certain periodicity—then fresh offerings have to be made. Of course these are offerings made out of fear, but what other choice is there?

Another form of magical flight is *flight through transformation*. In place of offerings, here we have transformation into various forms. An example of this is found in "The King's Son and the Devil's Daughter":[7] before he is born, the king's son is sold to the devil by his father, who is no longer capable of victory or of remaining in power through his own strength. There are similarities here with the initial situation in the tale of the black woman. The devil sets the king's son impossible tasks. If he fulfills them, he can then save his life; if not, he will once and for all be consigned to the flames. The demonic power demands a labor that goes far beyond human potential. The function of this is usually to make the arrogant consciousness give up, to force the hero to admit defeat and drop his motto: "Whatever I want, I can do." Usually in such situations the fairy tale hero lays his head in some girl's lap and goes to sleep. This means that now, psychically, he is at last capable of just letting things happen. The girl then accomplishes the tasks.

In our fairy tale, the devil's daughter, the "one with human feelings," as her father, the devil, calls her, accomplishes the task of her father's hostage. Only the third task, to build a church complete with dome and cross, is something hell spirits cannot do. Here only flight is possible. The devil's daughter changes herself into a white horse for the prince to ride. Every time the hell spirits get close, the pair transforms. She becomes a church and he the minister within it; then she becomes an alder tree and he the little bird perching in it; she becomes a field of brush and he the quail in it; she becomes a pond of milk and he the duck on it, who must always swim in the middle and never look at the devil. But then he does the forbidden thing, and the milk begins to ferment. This bit of disobedience turns out to be quite fortunate, because the milk, which the devil, in the form of a goose, quite simply guzzles up along with the duck, begins to ferment in his stomach and the devil bursts. The king's son and the former devil's daughter now stand out in all their beauty.

Of essential importance in the pursuit is that the prince through all his transformations never listens to the hell prince but rather sees him first. "Look behind you—what's following us?" is always the devil's daughter's question. Not listening to him, not entering into contact with him, clearly means that one simply cannot approach evil or certain destructive complexes directly. One has to look the other way, away from what is in pursuit; but at the same time one must look inward, concentrating on one's own center. This is what seems to me to be expressed in the image of the duck in the middle of the pond that has to keep its head. He supposedly should not gaze at the devil; but, as it turns out, he is supposed to look just a little. The devil bursts, which means that this unassimilable destructive complex loses its compactness, and thus also its menace and danger for consciousness. Hence it is all a question of extricating oneself from a destructive complex, a destructive affect. Only with the greatest effort can ego-consciousness keep its distance.

It is not the case that when eveything looks hopeless that flight is always the right solution. Flight, especially transformational flight, can take the place of a particular phase of a quest. After all, the princess wins the prince here too, so there really seems to be little difference between this and a quest. One only has to know when to seek and when to flee. This is a question of accurately assessing the potentialities and limits of consciousness in its relationship to evil. One must see the specific situation clearly, rather than seeing what one would like to see or what is "normally" seen under the circumstances.

That good always triumphs over evil in fairy tales is too crude a perception. It is not good that triumphs but the hero. And the hero is not only good. Good and evil stand opposed to each other and challenge each other. When the challenge can be taken up, usually both emerge from the adventure transformed. What triumphs, if it may be so expressed, is the drive for development. Nevertheless, in my view, one should not regard evil as too harmless. Even though the overarching event that a fairy tale describes usually encompasses some kind of development, nevertheless, individual situations can definitely be experienced as highly unpleasant, even as hopeless, with all the attendant fear and desperation. It is certainly unpleasant to be hexed by a witch, for example, and to have to go around looking and behaving like an animal. Nor is it easy to bear being turned into stone. It is not simple to have to run from the devil, whether he crops up in an individual or in a group. The devil always has great power—and no matter how much that power is condemned, it still lures us.

Fairy tales show us that confrontation with evil brings transformation. It transforms the hero and his entire life situation, and it transforms evil itself. It is precisely this hope for transformation that makes it possible to look evil in the face.

The ethic represented by fairy tales is an ethic of the path, the way. Acting spontaneously, the hero engages himself both with the situation at hand and the achievement of a goal. This activity is not merely good; its virtue is that it enables the hero to stay on the "path," on the way to the goal.

Thus fairy tales exhibit various forms of dealing with evil:

1. *Respecting evil* is the fundamental condition in any approach toward dealing with it. Here one acknowledges one's fear of evil, while allowing it a place in one's life and experience. This approach is used by Hanscarl Leuner in his catathymic image experiencing, a daydream technique that includes a "principle of nourishment." The idea is that by nourishing frightening figures in the imagination, one comes to experience them as being less fearful.

2. One can address oneself to the positive aspect within evil, for example, to the devil's grandmother. While this approach does discover destructive features in the adversary, it simultaneously engages the nondestructive side of him or her.

3. Seeing evil, but not falling prey to an inflation with it means stubbornly distancing oneself from the evil. One suffers and through this learns to accept that although the evil is stronger, one can nonetheless liberate oneself from it. This approach is definitely applicable wherever one is tangling with something that is stronger than the ego-consciousness.

4. Combat at the right moment can lead to the goal. This is an approach that is very familiar to us.

5. Trickery in dealing with evil often brings progress. Being able to make use of trickery presupposes that one has experienced evil within oneself and understood and accepted it. Only this makes possible the empathic insight into the strategy of the adversary that is necessary to be able to undermine it through trickery.

6. If evil is too strong, one can only *flee*. Here it seems essential to keep to oneself and avoid any major rapprochement with evil. To try to integrate evil in such a situation, as in a shadow-integration, would lead to catastrophe. Here we might think, for example, of situations in therapy when people show a very strong resistance to working with a problem. Perhaps the problem is stronger than their integrating ego-consciousness, at least in the current situation.

In fairy tales, the existence of evil is taken for granted. In this, they convey the idea that where there is evil, there is also always hope. One need only take the right approach. The tale of the king's son and the devil's daughter is a good example. Though evil is present, embodied by the devil, at the same time and in the same house, we have his daughter, who helps to overcome evil (who is actually her own father). Nevertheless, we dare not forget that there is an evil here before which one can only flee.

Holding one's ground, overcoming, or fleeing—none of these alternatives is inherently superior; it is precisely the hero's task to determine the appropriate response to whatever evil is at hand.

NOTES

1. August Ey (ed.), *Harzmärchenbuch* (Stade, 1862).
2. J. Bolte and G. Polivka, *Anmerkungen zu den Kinder- und Hausmärchen der Brüder Grimm*, vol. 2 (Hildesheim: Olms, 1963), pp. 231ff.
3. *Ungarische Volksmärchen* (Munich: Diederichs Verlag, 1966), p. 36.
4. *Märchen aus dem Donaulände* (Jena, 1926). In the original German, the phrase "the black woman" (*die schwarze Frau*) is not meant to refer to a person of African descent, as the English would suggest. —Editor
5. *Deutsche Märchen seit Grimm* (Munich: Diederichs Verlag).
6. *Balkan Märchen* (Munich: Diederichs Verlag).
7. *Deutsche Märchen seit Grimm*.

VERENA KAST

Methodological Remarks on Fairy Tale Interpretation

In interpreting a fairy tale text, one should take into account the possible levels, phases, and modalities of the interpretation. Basically, any fairy tale can be interpreted on two levels: collective and individual. Four phases always stand out in the course of the narrative: initial situation, intensification, turning point, and concluding situation; these mark the process of psychic transformation. The individual images as well as the imaginal context can be symbolically interpreted in a general or specific fashion. Finally, different modalities in dealing with the images are possible: in addition to the symbolic modality, there is also the meditative one.

O bviously, there are different types of fairy tale interpretation. Each is affected by the person interpreting, the historical situation, and the aims of the interpretation.

We interpret with the intention of pointing out parallels to psychic processes that are typical. These processes can occur again and again with different people; it is for this reason that they have also taken form and been preserved in fairy tales. What is important for us in making our interpretations is to translate their language into a form that allows us to recognize their message. Reading or listening to a fairy tale has an immediate emotional effect on us. Understanding a fairy tale by working with it in more depth adds new perspectives to that immediate effect. It would be rewarding and interesting to apply *all* the interpretive methods to a single fairy tale in order to find out what basic structures are common. But since this is often impossible in practice, we usually have to depend on only one method of interpretation.

The interpretive method employed in analytical psychology is based on the fundamental premise that fairy tales are an expression of the collective unconscious and thus present typical responses to typical human problems. These responses and expressions come from the creative aspect of the unconscious.

This premise gives rise to the different possible *levels* of fairy tale interpretation.

1. Interpretation as the description of how the fairy tale compensates for the deficiency of a collective situation, that is, how the situation is brought to completion and outgrown. Here it is more rewarding to see and interpret this growing-beyond as a process relating to a prevailing situation of consciousness than to place undue emphasis on the particular situation of consciousness itself.

In a second step, the collective situation in the fairy tale can be transposed onto a current collective situation. Typical human problems are constellated again and again. Fairy tales that deal with a current problematic are meaningful for more people than other fairy tales.

2. Collective processes are experienced differently by each individual; in that way, collective problems are also individual problems. We can also see the problems and their solutions shown in fairy tales as difficulties and possibilities in relation to the solution of individual problems. Here it is important to remember that we first transpose the entire action of a tale onto a psychic process and then in a second step apply it to an actual current problem.

A criterion for any successful interpretation is, as already discussed in the opening chapter, that one be able to maintain the interpretive approach one has chosen through the entire text. Basically, any interpretation is tenable that constitutes a whole with meaningfully related parts. In other words, interpretations are not tenable if they do not make visible an integral flow of action. It is in the nature of fairy tales that specific situations give rise to quite specific courses of behavior, which in turn can lead to quite specific solutions. In this, among other things, we see the practical use of fairy tales and their interpretation for therapeutic methodology. This becomes clear in applying the technique of active imagination. Active imagination means letting images arise in oneself and observing their transformations. We are pretty sure that when, in the course of such an imagination, we are pursued by a wild animal, we must try to get it on our side, for example, by giving it something to eat. Then it loses its menacing character. From where do we know this? From fairy tales, of course.

Over the course of action in a fairy tale, events occur in predictable phases that intensify until they reach the turning point. The following phases in this development are especially clear:

1. Initial situation: This is the existing condition that brings about the story to begin with. The initial situation is an image of the problem at hand that the fairy tale is going to work with.

2. Intensification: This is the way that leads to the turning point. It is often actually represented in the fairy tale as a road that the hero has to travel. In some cases, various turning points can already be found within this intensification phase.

3. Turning point: This can be recognized by the fact that another kind of behavior occurs after it. It is the moment in which the transformation that was being prepared by the intensification becomes manifest. The transformation proves itself real through a change in the action.

4. Concluding situation: An entirely new situation emerges as a result of this transformation.

If we take these phases into account in an interpretation that also respects the various levels, we are still left with the possibility of interpreting the images in either a general or specific manner. It is often helpful to first try a general interpretation. This is, however, not fully satisfying. For example, in many fairy tales we find the image of someone sitting in a hollow tree. A general interpretation of this on a high level of abstraction might be: a state of inactivity or waiting. But this is not waiting by a river, nor on a mountain; this waiting takes place in a hollow tree. To arrive at a specific interpretation, the concrete image must be placed within a particular symbolic context. This could be done in the present example by emphasizing the tree's protective function, which can be associated with maternity. The hollowness of the tree also reminds us of death. In the past, coffins were sometimes constructed out of hollow trees. But since this cavity is also open, it is also possible to come out of it again, to be born, as it were. In terms of personal experience, this image expresses not only a feeling of protection and security, but also the feeling of being closed in and, connected with that, the necessity at some point of coming out again.

We are only able to interpret symbolically here because the language of fairy tales is a language of images. Going beyond the individual symbol, it is also possible to interpret the interrelation of all the symbols appearing in the tale as a symbolic web of meaning. This also serves to verify the accuracy of our interpretations of individual images. However, the imaginal language of the fairy tale always suggests a double mode of interpretation:

1. The above symbolic interpretation, which makes use of the method of amplification
2. Interpretation through meditation

In practice, these two methods complement each other very well. To interpret a fairy tale using meditation, we call to mind the images of the tale and, disregarding for the moment their symbolic content, note the images arising in our mind in reaction to these images. This is a very individual sort of interpretation. We would only use this method on those fairy tales that have an immediate personal effect on us.

This meditative fashion of working with fairy tales is a good preparation for symbolic interpretation using the method of amplification developed by C. G. Jung. This essentially consists of compiling parallels from other fairy tales, mythologies, ethnological contexts, and so on. In this way, the meanings of a symbol that are common to all of these can be seen.

PART TWO

Evil in Fairy Tales

VERENA KAST

Thirty

Working with Repressed "Giant Affects"

This fairy tale is primarily about how to deal with so-called evil in our culture, with "giant affects" such as aggression, fear, and anger. This tale shows that these affects, along with the feminine principle (here there is not one woman to counterbalance thirty men) in a male-defined society, are split off from consciousness (taking the form of a giant's thirty daughters). The repressed feminine principle has taken on witchlike characteristics. Nevertheless, as the tale passes through its phases and the hero continues working on the affects, we see the undifferentiated emotions developing into feelings that are related to others. Energies that were exiled in emotions remote from consciousness become, in the course of the fairy tale, accessible within the realm of relationship.

There was once a man who had thirty sons. He had enough for them to eat and drink and often said: "When you all are out of school, I'll buy you each a horse. Then you can go out into the world and see for yourselves how to earn your bread."

He had named all the boys by numbers so he could tell them apart. The last and youngest of them was called Thirty. When he got out of school, he reminded his father of his promise, and the old man bought thirty horses, gave each boy money for his purse, and let them set out.

Although Thirty was the youngest of the brothers, he

47

nevertheless led them all, and they rode happily and contentedly along their way. In the evening they came to the house of a giant. They knocked on the door and asked: "Can we stable our horses here and stay for the night?"

The giant consulted his wife, and since he had no less than thirty daughters, he thought the boys would make a tasty morsel for his children. He had his wife tell them from the window: "Put your horses in the stable and come right in!"

They all went in, had a good dinner, and lay down to sleep. But they had to sleep in the same room as the giant's daughters, and the giant's wife put a black nightcap on every boy's head. But the giant's daughters had white nightcaps.

The brothers soon fell asleep. Only Thirty stayed awake. At a certain moment, he heard a knife being sharpened in the kitchen. "Woe are we!" he thought. "The giant plans to slaughter us." Then it occurred to him that the giant would be able to tell the black hats from the white even in the dark. Quickly, he jumped out of bed and exchanged the hats, so that now the brothers were wearing the white hats and the giant's daughters the black ones. Then he got back into bed and lay quite still. Meanwhile, the giant was still sharpening his knife. Finally, he heard the fellow say to his wife: "Now it's sharp enough to split a hair. Come, woman!"

Thirty kept still as a mouse as the giant came into the room and went from one bed to the other cutting the throats of everyone with black hats. He was glad when everything was quiet again. He woke his brothers and softly told them what danger they had been in.

Very carefully they slipped into their clothes, climbed out the window, untied their horses, and rode away into the pitch black night.

The following day, they came to thirty crossroads. At these they separated, each riding his own way.

Thirty rode along a road through the woods and came in the evening to the house of a witch. The door was open and he saw the old witch sitting by the hearth. Next to her was a tomcat with his tail held straight in the air. Thirty knocked at the door and the witch stood up from her stool and hobbled to the door. Thirty asked her if he could spend the night. She said, "You can stay with me forever and I'll give you my beautiful daughter for your wife if you are able to fulfill four wishes!"

Thirty asked to see the daughter. She was as beautiful as daylight, and the boy liked her so much that he said: "I will fulfill the four wishes!"

He went to sleep, and the next morning the witch told him the first wish. "You must fetch me," she said, "the carpet that the giant and his wife sleep on!" Thirty agreed and rode as fast as he could to the giant's house. He waited in the bushes until the giant and his wife went out. Then he snuck into the house and hid under the couch.

In the evening before going to sleep, the giant's wife said to her husband, "Come help me shake out the carpet we sleep on." She went and got the carpet and the giant helped her shake it out. Then they spread it on the floor, and the giant put out the light. But in the meantime, Thirty quickly rolled the carpet up, crawled away under the couch, climbed out through the window, and got away on his swift steed. The giant and his wife began to quarrel, because they each thought the other had pulled their part of the carpet away. Finally, they put the light on and saw that the carpet had been stolen. When Thirty got to the witch's house with the carpet, the witch was very happy. She praised Thirty highly and permitted her daughter to give him a kiss.

The next day the witch made her second wish. "You must," she said, "fetch me the giant's steed!"

"Nothing could be easier!" said Thirty, who got on his horse, and set out straight for the giant's house. First he waited till the giant had gone out into the woods, then boldly went in to the giant's wife and asked her if he could put his horse in her stable and stay for the night in her house. The giant's wife said: "Yes, just stable your horse and come in." Then Thirty went into the giant's stable, untied his horse, and rode away like the wind.

He arrived safe and sound at the witch's house. The witch praised him highly and permitted her daughter to give him two kisses.

The next day, the witch made her third wish. "You must fetch met the giant's parrot!"

"That I'll do," said Thirty with confidence, and off he rode.

He tied his horse to a tree in the woods, then snuck up to the giant's house. His luck was good and he was able to get into the giant's room through the window. But as he reached for the parrot, it cried out: "Thirty! Thirty!" The giant's wife came running out of the kitchen and grabbed him. She put him in a big wicker basket and said: "So now I have you! Now we'll fatten you up so you'll make a good meal!"

So there was poor Thirty in the basket. He got plenty to eat, and every day he got fatter. When the day before the feast arrived the giant's wife lugged in a huge quantity of wood. Thirty watched her as she painfully labored to split it small enough for the fire. Then he said: "Let me out of my cage for a while. I'll help you split the wood." The giantess laughed: "Ha, that would suit you fine, wouldn't it? Then you'd be able to run away." Thirty replied: "You can tie my feet together and fasten the rope to the bedpost." The giantess thought this over and said: "All right." She tied his feet together and knotted the rope to the bedpost. Then she gave him an axe. But as she bent over to toss him a bundle of wood, Thirty hit her on the head with the axe and she fell down dead. Then with one blow he loosed his feet from their bonds, grabbed the parrot, fetched his horse, which the giant had put in his stable, and hurried away.

When he arrived at the witch's house, he recounted his adventure. The witch praised him more than ever and permitted her daughter to give Thirty three kisses.

The next day, the witch made her fourth wish. "You must," she said, "bring the giant himself here to me alive!"

"I'm sure to pull that off!" said Thirty and set off on the road.

When he came to the giant's house, he saw the giant sitting despondently on the doorstep. Thirty got off his horse and boldly went up to him. He asked him why he was so sad, and the giant told him that he had killed his own children, his wife was dead, and now he could do nothing more clever than die himself.

When Thirty heard that, he said: "Yes, well in that case you should have a nice coffin." The giant asked: "Can you make one?" And when Thirty said yes, the giant was quite happy. Thirty went and got planks and worked like mad the whole day through. At last the coffin was ready. Then he said to the giant: "Now we have to try it out to see if it fits you." Artlessly, the giant lay down in the coffin and Thirty put the lid on and nailed it shut. Then he loaded the coffin in front of him on his horse and in this way brought the giant to the witch alive. Now the witch praised him beyond all bounds and said: "Now you shall have my daughter for your wife!" Then Thirty could have as many kisses as he wanted. The wedding was celebrated, and if Thirty hasn't died, then he is still alive today.[1]

There exist many fairy tales parallel to "Thirty." One of the best known is the Swiss fairy tale "Tredeschin."[2] "Thirty" is also composed of many well-known fairy tale motifs. We know the motif of exchanging caps from "Thumbling" (Grimm's no. 37); there is the Hansel and Gretel motif (Grimm's no. 15), motifs from "The Master Thief" (Grimm's no. 192), and in places the tale reminds us of "Faithful Ferdinand and Faithless Ferdinand" (Grimm's no. 126).

For the initial situation, we have a man with *thirty* boys, for whom he has enough to eat and drink. In other versions, there are only thirteen boys. In any case, we have an abundance of maturing males. Things are happening on quite a grand scale. In comparable stories, we usually have at most *three* boys who set forth into the world.

Obviously, this is not a situation of deficiency. The father only wants to get his sons off his back at some point, which is very understandable considering how long it must actually have taken to reach the point where the thirtieth son has finally grown beyond school age. They do not even seem to notice that there are no women around! Thus the challenge will be for the thirty to develop into individuals and for the feminine principle to be found.

The problem is that there are *so many* of them. (It is fitting that each son has only a number for a name—in a certain respect, each one is nothing more than a quantity.) Aside from this, however, things are not at all bad for them. They each get a horse and some money. Thus they are well outfitted, but the status quo can no longer be maintained. The number thirty might have some connection with this: three times ten brings a dynamic element into the picture. And Thirty (he is really the thirty-first) leads the way, creating the new development: he wants to go out and become independent.

The first thing the thirty sons come to after their departure is the house of a *giant*. This is not so surprising—where else would there have been enough space? But here we encounter the reverse situation: at the beginning we had an exclusively male society; now we find the complement for that in the thirty girls (thirty-two giants altogether if we count the giant parents, a slight numerical advantage). Clearly these women have been "repressed" up till now, because the men had to ride an entire day in order to reach them.

This house of giants with its giant daughters shows to what extent a "giant complex" is at work within the realm of the feminine. These are not just girls that they find there, they are a giant's daughters. This could be the expression of two things. First, matters that are repressed tend to expand to greater dimensions, becoming gigantic. Fear of them makes these repressed contents still more gigantic. Second, we must look into what giants symbolize in terms of content. From fairy tales we know that they are very strong and at the same time extraordinarily stupid. They always do everything with brute force. They are extremely irritable and simply rip apart in fury everything that gets in their way. From a psychological point of view, they might also betoken unstructured affects (giant anger, giant fear)—in our case, completely destructive affects.

This initial situation can then be interpreted on different levels, collective and individual.

Collective: A society that has heavily emphasized masculine qualities splits off and divorces itself from the feminine principle, especially insofar as emotions are concerned. Or perhaps it has not yet even discovered the feminine. We should note that nonetheless this bunch of men seems to be quite vital. Now the business at hand is to discover this "giant side" of the psyche.

Individual: In terms of an individual, we would have to think of a very vital, many-sided, but still rather unconscious personality, who probably suffers from terrific emotional onslaughts (for example, fits of anger), because these giants, even when they are far away, nevertheless remain active. We must get to the bottom of these emotional attacks. The energy that is bound up with them must be made useful.

Perhaps we could take group psychology as a working basis. It is the problem of every group that emotions are very much strengthened in a group. At one and the same time this strengthens both the opportunities and the problem, since the emotions tend to be too unconscious and therefore block insight. It is therefore essential to look into these emotions and make them conscious.

But the giant is dangerous. He wants to kill the brothers and feed them to his daughters. These giant's daughters devour what is human. This is a very appropriate image in view of the fact that in the throes of very strong emotions we often become inhuman. But the giant's dastardly intention is precisely the first step in getting this giant problem under control. The *giantess* herself devises the distinguishing sign: the sons have black caps, the giant's daughters white ones. On the face of it this is all it is—a distinguishing sign. But to me it seems of essential importance that a distinction is being made at all, because therein lies the first step in developing consciousness. The impulse for this comes from the giantess. Thirty, however, who really functions as an ego for his thirty brothers, goes even further. When he hears the knife being sharpened, he puts himself in the giantess's place and thinks as she would think. Thus he is able to use his imagination to learn what the giant is going to do next, and he anticipates his action. The secret to any strategy or trick is to think as the other person would think, for the most part in terms of their "evil" intentions, and then anticipate their action. In our tale, this means that Thirty definitely has a sense of his own giant nature. Being in the house of the giants also means having seen the dwelling place of this problem, *and knowing about it.* Through exchanging the nightcaps, however, the destructive fury of the giant is re-directed—not outward, against the boys, but inward, against his own flesh and blood. This results in the giant family being con-siderably reduced.

Perhaps we should interpret the role the colors black and white play as well. Among many other things, black is often con-sidered the color of guilt and death; white is connected with innocence. When we speak of seeing things in black-and-white terms, we mean making distinctions in an unsubtle way. By switching the caps, Thirty is of course saying that it is not they, the boys, who are the guilty ones. Thus the emotion of the giants is directed against their own children, but not against the one who has the emotion. On the personal level this would mean that though these unstructured emotions are to be seen as a problem in themselves, it does not follow that one should have guilt feelings about their existence.

Clearly the events in the giant's house make it possible for the thirty boys to separate—after they have first fled (in other words, distanced themselves). They can now enter upon *individual* paths, that is, become individuals. Thus this first experience consists in having found the giant's house, the locus of the giant complexes, and having evaded the destructive element connected with them by having distanced themselves from it. In this way, the complex has worked on itself internally. It is actually the case that in the throes of great emotions, we behave in an astoundingly collective fashion.

And now the tale shifts its focus to the story of Thirty—his brothers are of no further interest. As an individual, he has become more integrated just by the fact of having engaged the problem of emotion at all. Now Thirty encounters a witch, but one that is not all that witchlike. Nevertheless the tale does call her a witch. In itself, this is not surprising: he encounters the dark mother after the initial part of the story in which there were no women present at all. The repressed femininity has become witchlike. The witch is also willing to give him her daughter immediately if he can fulfill her four wishes. Thus the feminine element is to be attained on the personal level. Out of the emotions, feelings that are personal and related begin to emerge. Emotions as such are for the most part rather unrelated. But the feminine element is still in the witch's sphere of influence, that is, in the sphere of influence of a mother complex that has turned negative. The confrontation with the giant must be pursued further. In this phase, it is interesting that the witch has a very beautiful daughter and that the objects that must be fetched must come from the giant's house. Further confrontation with the giant in connection with winning the daughter means that now the emotions must be made workable in the realm of personal relationship. The tale stresses this point, for after each completed heroic feat, Thirty receives a precisely counted but increasing number of kisses.

These emotions hide within them a great deal that is essential; at the very least, an enormous amount of energy. When a guilt feeling arises, certain emotions are not allowed to exist. This causes the way to these energies to become obstructed. Chögyam Trungpa once remarked that all people have their own unique quality, maybe even a unique violence or laziness, and that this must be regarded as their particular characteristic quality rather than an error or blockage, for that is where their essential nature lies hidden.[3]

Let us now consider Thirty's individual feats of heroism. He is to fetch the carpet on which the giant and giantess sleep together. The carpet belongs to the giants and is at the same time their resting place, the place where they lie down and regenerate, a ground, a floor, a definitely circumscribed and also portable realm in which the two giants are to be found. In comparison to the house, the carpet is more body-related. If we assume that the giants embody giant emotions, then taking away the carpet would mean doing away with the narrow realm in which these emotions are accustomed to taking place, lifting it into consciousness. The giants no longer have the carpet—in other words, the emotions can no longer settle down on this ground.

How does Thirty approach this task? To begin with, he sneaks in. As soon as the carpet is rolled out but before it is occupied by the giant and giantess, Thirty pulls it away. The effect is not to give giant anger any room or ground to rest on. Anybody who has had a fit of anger knows how it can be intensified. We know exactly what kind of thoughts will make us even more furious. Pulling the carpet away would mean avoiding just this. And now the giants, in their giant way, get in a quarrel with one another and Thirty is able to get away. This phenomenon of the giants getting involved in mutual accusations should be seen in contrast to the possibility that they might immediately have turned outward. That is not what they do. *Emotion plays back into itself*—as it did before in the killing of the daughters; but here it is more centrally between the giant and the giantess. I see this as anger "stewing in its own juices," comparable with the situation in which someone is very angry, but the anger cannot be unleashed against any outsider. Angry internal dialogues are the result in which one realizes that the ego is actually hardly involved—it is really two giants arguing with each other. The argument is usually for the most part also correspondingly stupid. Recently in our civilization we have become accustomed to hearing that emotions should be expressed. And this is certainly correct; then the giants would not grow to such proportions. Nevertheless, we should make an important distinction: as long as *we* have the emotions, we should express them; but when the emotions have *us*, they no longer belong in the social sphere; they must be worked through internally beforehand.

After he has stolen the carpet, Thirty has to bring it to the witch. This witch is irritating. She is called a witch and is accompanied by a cat, as witches should be. On the other hand, she does not behave at all in a witchlike fashion other than in forcing Thirty to go back again and again to the giant. In other words, we have here a witch who is completely at the service of development. Such witches also appear now and then in other fairy tales. But it remains unclear whether Thirty really has to bring the things to the witch or whether, after he has completed the deed, they end up belonging to him. This is a significant distinction: If he is bringing them to the witch, then these objects and the energies bound up with them are closer to consciousness than before but remain in the witch realm rather than the realm of the ego. Put another way, the question we are really asking (by way of anticipation) is whether in the end he leaves the witch or stays with her. In this respect the other versions of the story are not entirely comparable. The one who sends Thirty, or whatever he is called in those versions, on his journeys no longer plays any role at the end of the story.

Before tackling this problem, let us turn our attention to the other heroic feats. Now Thirty has to go get the giant's steed, which he succeeds in doing without complication. In fact, however, he *exchanges his own steed for that of the giant.* Instead of his own steed, we should perhaps say his former steed. One's horse, as we have seen, can be understood in a quite general and comprehensive sense as a driving force. That the giant's steed is a swift one I conclude from the fact that the boy rides away like the wind. Taking it could mean seeing what great energies are buried in these giant emotions and claiming them for oneself. This would mean experiencing oneself not only as one who is embroiled in large emotions and is victimized by them, but also as one who through them is in possession of giant energies, energies that can be invested, for one thing, in relationships. As a sign of this, at this point Thirty receives three kisses.

Next Thirty has to get the parrot. We are struck by the self-confidence with which Thirty always sets out. Heroes have primordial confidence!

But with the parrot, things do not go so smoothly. Thirty must have been discussed often in the giants' house for even the parrot to know his name. After all, a parrot only parrots back what has been said in front of it. It is well known that parrots are generally very garrulous and repeat more or less mechanically whatever they have picked up. The parrot might well embody this kind of mechanical chatter or gossip, an impersonal, mechanical way of behaving that is characteristic of giant emotions. But now Thirty has blundered. The parrot sees him and he does not see the parrot. Otherwise he could have silenced it. Parrots should only be carried off when they are sleeping (cf. "Tredeschin"). On account of this, he once more gets caught in the giant's house.

In Persian tales, parrots are all-knowing and often act as advisors. In this tale as well, the parrot has the function of knowing what must be done. Thirty *must* be caught in the giant's house again in order to learn that further work on the giant problem is needed. We know this from analysis: a person falls back into a complex just at that moment when he feels he has begun to integrate it.

Thirty is going to be eaten up. That would mean the emotions gaining the upper hand—a serious matter. As sweetly as the story is written, it is nevertheless clear that one of the two sides, the giants' side or Thirty's side, has to yield. The two cannot continue to exist side by side. But now Thirty has come to a bad end—or so it appears. He obviously does not give up hope, and hence his position turns out once again not to be all that bad. Here we have a Hansel-and-Gretel passage: The giantess moves into the position of the witch, the *real witch* with her vicious circle: imprison, feed, devour. And Thirty proves that he can deal with witches. He offers the witch his help and also immediately tells her how she can prevent his getting away. He attunes himself to her desires and worries and allays the latter; he even pretends to be sympathetic. *He becomes active.* He treats the witch in the most charming way—and kills her, because he sees that he is really in for it, that the ego could be destroyed. In my opinion, as a symbol the parrot stands for taking pleasure in complaining, continuously repeating oneself, which, as we said, is characteristic of these emotions and can be quite pleasurable, a kind of mother-complex type of enjoyment. After all, in what follows he is also fed by the giantess. *And this very same giantess who first feeds and then devours he must kill.* Killing the giantess could mean killing his own lust for power, the feelings of power that arise out of the emotions, out of the pleasure taken in them. Thus he sacrifices the pleasure gained from these emotions, because otherwise he will remain captivated by them.

For his last feat, Thirty must bring the male giant to the witch alive. Unfortunately, nothing is said about what she intends to do with him.

The giant is sitting despondently on his doorstep. He wants to die. Once again Thirty attunes himself to the giant's intentions—he does not try to change his mind but seeks in the sphere of the giant's emotional state what will ultimately be useful to himself, what will advance his own ends. But he stays in the sphere of the giant's desire. This attunement to the desire of the giant in ourselves means tuning into what these disturbing emotions want from us.

The giant is sad because he has lost everything. And he recounts this to the very person who has been instrumental in bringing it all about. Because he has lost everything, he wants to die as well. The giant has now been rendered completely impotent, he has no more life force—in this sense the problem has been worked through. He is brought along—as a memento or as something still to be worked on?—into the next phase of life. He is brought along in a *coffin*. A coffin is closely related to a tree in one way and to a ship in another. In some places, a coffin is called a "tree of death." The idea behind this is that the deceased returns again to the protection of the mother. Insofar as this is the case, what we have here is a pacification of all of these giant emotions. They are delivered, as in a ship. However, the fact that the giant remains alive is an indication that the problem could flare up again and is only banished for the moment. Then we see that as a result of this last deed the personal relationship can claim its place: Thirty gets as many kisses as he wants. What is not clear, as already mentioned, is whether the witch remains present or Thirty is now alone with the witch's daughter, or perhaps even leaves. What is clear in any case is that the total energy that was present in the giant's household has now been delivered, made available to the realm of relationship.

I believe the main movement of the tale is this: To begin

with, we have a male society without women, followed by the emergence of repressed, prehuman emotions. (In accounts of the creation, the giants are always the generation before humans.) Through perception of this prehuman element, a gradual integration is achieved, primarily on the emotional level.

Of course every major complex that is split off has a giant emotion connected with it. In the collective situation, this means that many complexes combine. I have always kept to this relatively abstract level in working with giant emotions, because everything that is capable of possessing us really functions according to this pattern. This also goes, for example, for a giant demand that has been repressed.

This can apply to a single person or an entire society. One can take the same approach with group emotions. What seems to me important in this fairy tale and its variants is that the energy from the giant complex is delivered over into energy that can be invested in relationships. In general, strong complexes draw us out of relationships. Here relationships can be understood in a very broad sense, which could also include relationships to things and to work. Work-related disturbances are particularly clear examples of how complexes absorb so much energy that none is left for work. Appeals at this point to good will are ineffective, because the person involved is no longer capable of willing.

To work on one's complexes is thus also a social matter that brings a definite gain, as we can see by the many kisses that Thirty received step by step along his way.

NOTES

1. *Deutsche Volksmärchen* (Munich: Diederichs Verlag), p. 125.
2. "Tredeschin," in *Schweizer Volksmärchen* (Munich: Diederichs Verlag).
3. Chögyam Trungpa, *Meditation in Action* (Boston: Shambhala Publications, 1985), pp. 20–21.

VERENA KAST

The Cursed Princess
The Problem of Sadomasochism

*Ordinarily we encounter evil in daily life in patterns of be-
havior that disturb or even prevent relationships between
people. Fairy tales vividly portray these patterns of behavior
as curses. In contemporary terms, we could call them sadomasochistic. Behind such patterns, the imaginal language of
the following fairy tale shows us the figure of a mountain
spirit, an overelevated father figure under whose spell the
girl in the tale inwardly falls. Taking into account the individual as well as the collective level of the problem, this interpretation particularly focuses on the phase of liberation
from this complex, in the course of which a relationship between male and female partners becomes possible.*

There was once a father who had a son whose name was
Peter. The son was not happy at home, so he asked for his
inheritance, which was twenty talers, and set forth into the
wide world. The lad had a compassionate heart and a sense
of right and wrong, and he helped out wherever he could.

Once he came to the outskirts of a village where he
found a dead man lying on the ground. Not far away a
farmer was plowing. Peter went to the farmer and asked why
the man had not been buried. The farmer answered that the
dead man had been poor and the village had not buried him
because there was an expense involved. Thus he had been
brought to where he was, where the birds and foxes would
feed on him until in the long run there would be nothing
left. This made Peter feel sorry, and he immediately asked

what the burial would cost. The farmer answered. "Oh, about twenty talers."

Then Peter went to the village mayor, gave him twenty talers, and gave orders for the dead man lying on the edge of the village to be buried. And that is what happened. He himself stayed long enough in the village to accompany the corpse; then he traveled on.

When he had gotten out of the village and traveled a short stretch beyond it, a man came up behind him, struck up a conversation, and told him that he wanted to accompany him on his travels. Peter was pleased with this, for the man looked so good and upright that he immediately took to him and was glad to have found such a doughty traveling companion.

They had already traveled together for several weeks and each had already told the other what was in his heart when they came to a town where all the houses were hung with black cloth, and high above over the castle a black banner flew as a token of mourning. Peter asked what the reason was. The people told him that their dear, good princess had been bewitched by a mountain spirit. The whole day long she was quiet and withdrawn, but from time to time she flew into such a rage that she beat and killed whoever or whatever fell within her reach. Particularly, any man who dared to try to save her was doomed to death if he was unable to guess the riddle she set him. Many handsome princes had already met their death at her hands, and many other honest youths had lost their lives on her account. As a result, a year had passed since anyone could be found who would try to save her. And yet she had been such a kind and beautiful girl and still was.

Then Peter said to his companion: "Should I try my luck? What do you think? Do I dare? If I die, I would die in a good cause. If I succeed, there could be no greater good fortune for her and for me."

His companion said: "Go ahead, do it. I will help you.

And so you will know I am capable of it, I will tell you that I am not a human being but the spirit of the man you had buried in the village. I know ways enough for you to succeed in your purpose. So go to the king and tell him you want to save the princess. He will be very glad of it and will reward you richly if you succeed."

So Peter went to the king, had himself announced, and was let in to see him. When he had explained his intentions, the king said: "My dear young man, you are involving your-self in a difficult undertaking. Consider that it will cost you your life if you do not succeed in saving my daughter. She will kill you on the spot if you do not guess the riddle she sets you."

"That is of no matter," said Peter. "I will try, let it go with me as it may."

"Then come again tomorrow," said the king. "I'll tell my daughter."

Then Peter went back to his inn, where his companion was waiting for him. When he told him of the king's answer, his companion said: "Just wait till ten o'clock this evening; then I will take care of everything. Until then, tell no one what is on your mind and be of good cheer. You will save the princess, I'll see to it." Then they let it go at that.

They went out together and saw the town and everything of note that was there. They also learned where the princess lived and which windows were those of her bedchamber. They then returned to the inn, ate their evening meal, and passed the time talking until the stroke of ten.

Then Peter's traveling companion took a crock and a large pair of wings out of his knapsack and a very slender iron rod. Peter then had to take his clothes off. The spirit spread the salve that was in the crock on Peter's shoulders and put the wings on him. Then he said: "Now fly up to the princess's chamber window and watch for her to come out. Then keep beating her with the rod. Fly wherever she flies and whatever place she goes into, sneak in with her. Then creep out of sight and listen to what the mountain spirit says. She will tell him everything and then she will also ask him what she should set you for a riddle. Pay close attention and keep still."

When the wings had grown onto Peter, the spirit opened the window. "On the way back, you must follow the princess in the same way until she flies back into her window." Now Peter got the iron rod in his hand and flew through the window and out over the town to the princess's window. There he saw her. She also had wings on and was rushing back and forth in her room as though she did not have all her wits about her. He settled down on the sill and waited until she came out. As soon as the clock struck eleven, she opened the window and flew out. Peter flew after her and soon caught up; he began to beat her quite dreadfully so that he felt very sorry about it. But there was no other way. He had to obey, even if it made his heart bleed.

Finally they came to a big tall mountain, which opened up and they both flew in. "Now I have to be careful," Peter thought, and snuck into the great hall along with her. Near the door stood a big altar. He hid himself behind the altar so he could hear everything and yet get out fast if things went wrong or when the time came. The princess ran to the mountain spirit and he took her in his arms. He was an old man with a snow-white beard and had eyes in his head that glowed like fiery coals. His whole being was so wrathful and menacing that Peter was properly frightened and began to be sorry he was there. Nevertheless, he didn't stir, for he had no way of getting away. The door had disappeared and where it had been there was once again just rock.

At last the mountain spirit said to the princess: "Been a long time gone, a long time since you murdered someone, a long time since you feasted on the blood of your deliverer. Is there another bird in the net?"

"Yes," she answered, "another one has showed up, but just an ordinary man, not a prince, baron, or nobleman. But there is a raging, powerful hailstorm outside. See here, O high spirit, how I am torn and bruised from the hailstones," and the blood flowed from her.

"That is of no matter," said the mountain spirit. "Now you must torment your human victim all the more, you must take all the more pleasure in having his blood, you must drink all the more of it, and you will be pure for me and be my own all the sooner."

"But what should I set him as a riddle? What should I think of?" asked the princess.

"Think of your father's white steed," the mountain spirit replied.

"Good," said the princess and then she asked: "Let me out, for it is a quarter to twelve. I still have far to fly, as you know, and twelve o'clock arrives quickly." The mountain spirit made an opening and the princess departed with Peter behind her. Outside in the air she was beaten as before all the way to her chamber window. The princess flew in, and Peter flew home, took off his wings, and went to bed. His companion was already asleep, but had told him beforehand to remove the wings with care and return them to the knapsack, being careful not to bend a single feather. This Peter did, then slept until morning.

In the morning he got up, dressed himself handsomely, had an excellent breakfast with his companion, and set out for the castle. There he was brought before the princess. She was sitting in a beautiful chamber on a small sofa and looked quite troubled; but she was the most delightful maiden. Her gaze was so gentle and kind; she was not big and strong but finely and delicately fashioned. It was scarcely possible to believe that she had ever killed anyone. Nonetheless, nine men had already met their death at her hands.

As Peter entered her parlor, she immediately stood up, approached him, and said in a friendly manner: "So you wish to save me. But do you also know that it will cost you your life if you don't guess my riddle?"

"Yes," he said, "but I intend to try. If I must die, I will gladly die for you. You are so beautiful and kind and sweet that I will gladly face death for you. Tell me your riddle."

"So be it," she replied very sadly, and tears came to her eyes. She came closer to him and said, "I feel sorry for you, but since you won't have it any other way, listen: Tell me what I am now thinking of."

"That is not hard to say," Peter answered. "Princess, you are now thinking of your father's white horse."

The princess became pale as a corpse and said: "You have guessed it. May fortune continue to favor you. Come again tomorrow. If you set me free, you will be royally rewarded."

Peter bowed and departed. He again passed the day with his traveling companion and was in high spirits. In the evening, everything happened as it had the first time, except this time Peter received two iron rods, one in each hand, with which to thrash the princess. But when they came to the mountain and entered the hall, it was more brightly lit than the previous evening, and in the middle was the moon, shedding its light over everything. On the altar lay a big spiny fish. The previous evening there had been only a few stars in the ceiling, and the altar had been empty.

Now when the princess had entered and Peter had snuck in behind her, the door closed. The princess approached the mountain spirit, who was sitting on a kind of throne, and said: "O high spirit, the man has guessed our first riddle. What do you say to that?"

"There is more going on here than meets the eye. A mysterious power is at work that is hostile to you and me. This time think of your father's battle sword."

"Good," said the princess. "The flight has once again cost me a lot of blood. It is hailing even worse tonight than last night. See how I am bleeding. But if he does not guess the riddle, he will die by my father's battle sword. You can rely on that."

"So be it, my daughter. Now go and do what you must

do, but tell no one the riddle." And with that, off she went with Peter behind her.

On the way, she received her full share of blows, all the way back until she flew in at her window. Peter flew home, took off his wings, and went to bed. The following morning he went once again to the princess, and she received him just as on the previous day. This time, however, her father's battle sword already lay on the table, blood stains still on it. As he entered, she immediately asked, "What am I thinking of?"

"Of your father's battle sword, noble princess."

She sank back on the sofa and stammered, "You've guessed it! Come again tomorrow. May fortune be with you once more; then all will be well." Then Peter went off and brought his friend the news that he had guessed the second riddle as well.

The two passed an enjoyable day until darkness fell; then they ate together. When it was nearly ten o'clock, Peter's companion said: "Tonight you have a hard task before you. This time you will receive two iron rods with which you must scourge the princess and a two-edged sword with which you must cut off the mountain spirit's head. But be careful when you enter his hall that he doesn't see you, because this time it will be as bright as day in there, and it will be difficult to hide from him. I, however, will be with you, and if you get in trouble, I will protect you. Be of good courage. At the end he will accompany the princess out. When he has taken leave of the princess and is about to go back into the mountain, cut off his head and take it with you."

Everything happened just as his companion had said. Peter was waiting for the princess at her chamber window. At eleven she came out, and he went behind her and flogged her quite terribly all the way into the mountain. As they entered the great hall together, there was the sun on the ceiling, and everything was as bright as day. On the altar the spiny fish lay and a fiery wheel stood. But behind the altar all was dark, and Peter hid himself there immediately. The princess hurried to the mountain spirit, threw herself into his arms, and said as though in despair: "He has guessed again!"

"That is bad," said he. "This time think of my head. No mortal being could think of that, least of all a human."

"Oh," she cried, "how I have been flayed this time by the horrible hailstorm. Look at my back, my arms, my head. I am dripping with blood."

"I feel sorry for you, my child," said the mountain spirit. "This is a hard trial. Now go and bathe in the blood of the shameful one. I will be with you, count on me; tomorrow, though invisible, I will be by your side. This time he will not succeed in guessing the riddle."

Then he accompanied her out. As he was about to go back in, Peter cut off his head with one blow, grabbed it by the hair, and flew off after the princess, once more giving her a dire and thorough drubbing right up to her window. Then he went home, laid himself in the feathers, and rejoiced in advance about getting things his way. Once again, he slept very well and the following morning he got himself properly dressed, took the head of the mountain spirit, wrapped it in a kerchief, and went off to the castle.

When he entered the princess's room this time, the princess was all pale with fright and did not know whether she should tell the riddle or not. Then Peter said: "Noble princess, today I have come for the last time. Tell me your riddle so that I can guess it or die."

And the princess, her voice trembling as though her life or death depended on it, asked, "What am I thinking of?" Without answering, he untied the kerchief and put the head of the mountain spirit on her table. "My deliverer!" the princess cried out and collapsed into his arms in a faint. He laid her down on the sofa and rang for help. Servants soon arrived, and the king was fetched and the doctors too.

When the princess regained her senses, the king gave her to Peter as his wife. Peter replied that before anything else he had to return to the inn. A great coach with six horses harnessed to it was immediately prepared and Peter was driven to the inn. His companion met him at the coach door, helped him out, and together they went upstairs to their room. There the traveling companion said to Peter: "When you are about to go to bed with your wife, without her knowing, set a large tub of water next to the bed, so that when she jumps up that night and wants to go out, she will land in the tub of water. You must immediately push her under. A raven will emerge from the tub and fly away. Then push her under again, and a dove will come out and perch on your shoulder. Then push her under again, and the princess in her former angelic beauty and goodness will climb out of the tub. Then kiss her three times and be happy with her. After the death of the old king, you will become king. Now farewell; you no longer have need of me; I leave you now and the world as well. I believe I have repaid you my debt. Farewell and be happy!" Then he disappeared.

Peter got into his coach, very sad about parting from his companion, and drove back to the royal palace. There he faithfully followed all his companion's instructions and everything happened as he had been told. He was as happy as a king with his wife, and later he actually became king and governed his country well until he came to a peaceful end.[1]

"The Cursed Princess" is divided into two parts. The first part deals with releasing the spirit of a dead man, the second with the liberation of a princess who is possessed by a mountain spirit, a deed that can only be accomplished with the help of this dead man. At the end we have our Peter with his once again peaceful princess, and we know that later he will be king. Both the dead man's spirit and the mountain spirit are gone. But the second part of the tale is unthinkable without the first. Thus we will have to pay special attention to these spirit figures, even though they drop out of the narrative at the end, which indicates that the problematic they represent has to a certain extent been worked through.

In looking at the unfolding of this story, we see that what we have here is a long tale of liberation or release. Peter frees himself from his father. He frees the dead man from his state of unrest. The dead man's spirit helps Peter to solve the riddles—that is, to get free of their grip, which in turn frees the princess from the mountain spirit, who himself had to be superseded and freed. By helping to bring this about, the spirit of the dead man is released from his debt. At the end, both Peter and the princess have been released: Peter from the grateful spirit of the dead man and the princess from the mountain spirit.

The overall theme of this fairy tale is thus one of gaining freedom from fathers and the father spirits who stand immediately behind them. Through this process, our hero gains his independence and, moreover, gains a wife—or a feminine part of himself that once again functions in a satisfactory or liberated fashion. If we interpret this in terms of the feminine psyche—and in my view there are good grounds for doing so—it would mean that the woman is freed from the clutches of a dominating father figure who is causing her significant psychological difficulties.

This would be the general interpretation. Now let us turn to the details. Peter does not like life at home. He goes off, taking his entire inheritance with him. He separates from his father because he no longer likes being with him. His unhappiness is a starting point for something new that has to be developed. Since there are no women in the initial situation, we can assume that he is going to be involved with finding a woman. It is curious how respectable and proper Peter is portrayed as being. As the tale goes on, we are continually reminded of his good qualities. In his travels, he runs across an unburied dead man. This poor dead man is one who during his life never made much money and thus was not respected or cared for. In this way he embodies the shadow aspect, a side of the psyche that is not lived out even though it would like to participate. What could it be that has been repressed so? From the story, we only know that this dead man was so poor that he could not be buried. Parallel versions of the tale tell us more. In one case the figure was a sinner whom the church denied burial. In another version, he was a debtor. In the Norwegian fairy tale "The Companion," he was a wine dealer who diluted his wine. These characters all have human failings of a sort that we can hardly imagine would merit the denial of burial rights. They are simply figures who do things good people do not do.

Nevertheless, in all cases, the hero needs all the money he got from his father to redeem this dead man. All the values left over from his old attitude have to be sacrificed in order to bury the dead man and lay this problem "to rest." The meaning of this is that he has accepted the shadow side and given up a lot to do so—at the very least the old image that he had of himself, in this case the image of "my father's good son." And of primary importance is the fact that after this the companion and the hero travel a common path, become friends, and arrive together in the town where the king's daughter lives. We learn from the continuation of the story that the traveling companion is the spirit of the dead man. Thus a long way had to be traveled in order for Peter to become friends with this spirit; and it is only with this spirit that it is possible for him to save the princess. The two sides of this companion are clearly shown: on one hand, there is the disgraced side of the dead man; on the other, once he has been accepted, he becomes a helper. This helper is also shown to have a connection to something very deep, for he can do much more than any ordinary man. In a Finnish version, he is even portrayed as an angel of God. What is important here is that he is connected to something that is far beyond consciousness.

Now both of them arrive in the town, which is draped in black, a town in mourning. Things have come to something of a standstill at the king's court. Nevertheless, it is learned that the "sweet, kind princess" is under the spell of a mountain spirit. Just how this spell is manifested is very clearly portrayed: most of the day she is quiet and withdrawn, but from time to time she flies into a rage and smashes to pieces whatever comes her way. Whoever wants to save her but does not solve her riddle is killed[2]—obviously by her own hand. We are told that the princess was such a kind and beautiful girl, and still is; her eyes are gentle and kind and she is fine and delicate—nevertheless she has killed nine men. Now a year has passed since the last victim and how it is the tenth man's turn. This description gives us the feeling that in a certain respect the girl may have been too sweet, fine, and gentle. Though this is no longer her problem, her present condition is by no means satisfactory. The story tells us she is bewitched; it seems that the nature of the mountain spirit speaks through her. Her psychological condition could be described as depression (symbolized by the town draped in black) alternating with blind rage and aggressive outbursts. Lacking any freedom of will in the whole process, she is a prisoner of the situation. The fact is that at the same time she both wants and does not want to be liberated. To me it seems that both tendencies exist side by side in more or less equal strength. Thus she has tears in her eyes when she gives him the riddle, saying to him: "I feel sorry for you"; then after he has guessed it she becomes pale as a corpse. We have the impression of a very refined, impressionable, rather depressive person, who can suddenly burst into a fury, and who in this fury does not shrink from being extremely harmful. Not just harmful—lethal. Her fury seems to be endlessly destructive.

This is more or less comparable to those states in which a person is suddenly overwhelmed by a very destructive mood, and becomes capable of destroying in a very short time a human relationship that has been built up over years. Above all, such moods are self-destructive. The princess must be saved from these states—and the spirit of the dead person knows how to go about that. Not only does he have the necessary knowledge to give Peter, he also has the means—the wings. Since the princess must surely have received her wings from the mountain spirit, this shows that the spirit of the dead man and the mountain spirit are not all that different. Both are called a "spirit," which may mean that they are two aspects of the same spirit.

It is interesting how Peter simply obeys this spirit, even in a situation as unfamiliar to human beings as flying. This could be due to an early bond he had with his father. It is essential for him to do exactly what the princess does, follow her and take her errant ways—if that is what they are—on himself. Moreover, he has to beat her with iron rods (in the beginning, one is enough). The tale says, "He had to obey, even though it made his heart bleed." Thus he has to be aggressive and in this way, he takes on part of the aggression. This seems to me an important aspect of this business with the rods. And this is increased step by step each day.

And now both of them arrive inside the big mountain. The mountain spirit obviously lives there underground, a symbol for being cut off from the brightness of day, for whatever is inside the mountain is hidden. In this mountain there is an altar in a hall. One has the impression of a church within the mountain and this lends the mountain spirit a sense of importance. He looks so terrifying that Peter is frightened of him. This suggests that just a glimpse of the demonic power behind the princess's destructive nature—whether this is the feminine side of Peter or a woman who is possessed by a mountain spirit—makes one want to flee in terror. But the princess runs to the arms of this demon. For her, the situation seems to possess some kind of grandeur. It is not his dwelling alone that gives us evidence of the nature of this mountain spirit, but also what he says. "Been a long time gone, a long time since you murdered someone, a long time since you feasted on the blood of your deliverer. Is there another bird in the net?" Here we hear triumphant, sensual gratification in killing—and especially in killing those who want to free the princess. The spirit feels strong and superior to anyone who wants to save her. And when the princess complains of the hailstorm, of the tortures she has had to bear, he only says, "That is of no matter. Now you must torment your human victim all the more, you must take all the more pleasure in having his blood, you must drink all the more of it, and you will be pure for me and be my own all the sooner." The more you suffer, the more you must make others suffer. This is the psychology that he represents. But not only that; she must take pleasure in this. We have here, and I will come back to this later, the quintessence of a sadomasochistic style of behavior. I use the expression *sadomasochistic* to describe a situation in which torturing and being tortured is bound up with a certain experience of pleasure, but not necessarily sexual pleasure. This is not related to the sexual sphere in an exclusive way at all.

Freud in his conception of a "moral masochism"—offering one's cheek wherever one might hope to catch a slap, and not only from one's lover—had already moved away from the strictly sexual sense of the term. "The more you suffer, the more you have to make others suffer, and take pleasure in it." But the mountain spirit continues, significantly: "All the more will you become my own—pure for me." Not only will she take pleasure in this suffering, her bondage to it and to the mountain spirit will deepen as long as she remains in this circular pattern of behavior. For in fact she only seeks out the mountain spirit when someone comes to save her. As long as no one is trying to save her, she apparently does not. It is crucial that Peter is present to overhear this scene between the mountain spirit and the princess, for then her isolation is no longer so complete. This means that though her bondage to this spirit still persists, someone now knows about this bondage and therefore it is no longer total.

And now the riddle. She is to think of her father's white horse. This laconic question "What am I thinking of?" may be more revealing than it first seems, especially if we take into account the other objects that she is supposed to think of. There is her father's white horse, and his battle sword, and then the head of the mountain spirit, who in the meantime has addressed her as his daughter. This princess who is of marrying age has her father's things—and her spirit father's things—very much on her mind. This suggests an intimate paternal bond, which harmonizes well with the fact that in this fairy tale we hear nothing of a queen at the royal court. If she is there, she plays no role. On the whole, the situation seems tremendously patriarchal. But why is it particularly her father's *white horse* that crops up? In mythology, white horses are horses of the sun. They are connected with the god of light and embody his energy. By contrast, dark horses are horses of the god of the underworld. Horses in themselves symbolize instinctive energy—impulsive, instinctive energy. To me it seems that, taken broadly, her focus on her father's white horse is more than simply an expression of attachment to him. There is also a sense of breaking loose here, connected with the positive aspect of the paternal bond. It is almost as though the mountain spirit himself also wants somehow to be saved, released. After all, it is he who comes up with this riddle. Being saved here would mean no longer being so split off, no longer being a monster. But let us not be too optimistic, though this horse symbol does suggest spring, and it is in fact spring when someone finally comes who is equipped to break this curse. The horse symbol also seems to me to convey that there is considerable libido bound up with this attachment to the father, libido that could be used to make some progress in the situation.

Now it is time for Peter to solve the riddle. At this point the princess becomes tearful and sentimental, which at first glance does not seem consistent with her brutality, but in the fairy tale the two go hand in hand. Thus she asks him in a kindly tone if he realizes that this could cost him his life. This reminds me of people who reassure us at length that they could never hurt anyone, and then very skillfully do something quite brutal. We are left there with the reassurance that we should not take this as an injury, but feeling all the same we have been seriously hurt. We also might have wanted to strike back if our hands had not been tied by so many reassurances. The fact that the princess becomes as pale as a corpse when Peter guesses the riddle fits well with this interpretation.

Now comes Peter's second flight to the mountain spirit, his second journey to find out what the princess is thinking, that is, what her secret is. She is beaten even more than before—Peter must now be even more aggressive. And the tale no longer refers to his feeling sorry for her. These beatings are an expression of how much the princess must suffer on the way to the mountain spirit. Her journey there must be made punishing, so that it becomes quite difficult for her to take this particular path. This reminds us of exorcism scenes in the New Testament in which the evil spirits complain of being tormented by Christ.

In everyday terms, this could mean that when we sense a destructive undertow in others we should react aggressively, not scornfully, but with the sense of participation suggested by Peter's accompanying the princess on her journey. One thing one can accomplish in this way is to absorb the other person's aggression, because he or she is not left the only one angry; in addition, such a reaction develops a sense of the "world of the mountain spirit" in the other person—a sense of its destructiveness.

This time it is brighter in the hall—the moon is there. The previous evening there had only been a few stars. If this is a church, it would seem to be a nature church. The increasing brightness suggests that the whole complex situation is susceptible to being illuminated. One can see better, and it is not by artificial but by natural light.

On the altar is a big spiny fish. Such objects help us to identify the mountain spirit more definitely. He appears as a power that is related to the cosmos, to the sun, moon, and stars, which gives him a universal character. Then we have the further addition of a spiny fish. Fish have a highly complex symbolism, but I will confine myself to their most general sense. They are what live in bodies of water; they swim around and people try to pull them out. This one has obviously already been pulled out. We might say that a fish has been drawn from the unconscious. But just as we may only know what we have caught when we eat it, so here we are not yet sure what may lie hidden in this fish. Sometimes we know we have gotten hold of something but cannot quite yet grasp the content—the spines confirm this. Fish with spines are unpleasant to take hold of. In former times, altars were hearths, the place where things were cooked. Thus the altar is the place where things are transformed. But in this context the fish's spininess could also mean that the whole problem is a spiny problem, which it doubtless really is. This is no saving grace that has come out of the unconscious; rather it something one pricks one's hands on.

The spirit is sitting on the high throne. He has to do this, for if there is a mysterious power hostile to him and the princess, he must elevate himself so as to emphasize his omnipotence.

Though the princess's deliverance is already in progress, it is possible for her condition to become more destructive. This is shown by the fact that when Peter makes his second visit, she does not get involved in any long preliminaries. She goes straight for her goal—beheading! The battle sword, the subject of the riddle she poses to Peter, is already lying on the table. Here we get the very strong impression of someone who is possessed. She can wait no longer. The battle sword is the sword with which her father achieves his victories and slays his enemies. If she kills her deliverer with her father's battle sword, she does not kill him with her own means; rather she shows her dependency on her father. It is not her aggression but her father's aggression. And as Peter guesses her thought, she falls back on the sofa and stammers: "You've guessed it! Come again tomorrow. May fortune be with you once more; then all will be well." Throughout the text, this ambivalence is maintained. It must, in my view, be maintained, because the princess has an ambivalent feeling about her deliverance. On the one hand, she is possessed and is thus incapable of wanting to be free of the possession; on the other hand, there is a desire to get on with life, and for this the possession must be broken. Possession works like a straitjacket; it keeps one from getting on with life.

On his third journey to the mountain spirit, Peter takes a sword with which he is supposed to cut off the mountain spirit's head. Up till now, it has been the princess who has cut off the heads of her unfortunate would-be rescuers; now Peter undertakes this in relation to the mountain spirit, after beating the princess once again, as instructed. The companion who prepares Peter is extremely well informed. It is interesting that both he and the mountain spirit utter sentences of exactly the same meaning: "I, however, will be with you, and if you get in trouble, I will protect you," says the companion. "I will be with you, count on me; tomorrow I will be by your side, though invisible," says the mountain spirit. This shows that there is certainly an affinity between the two spirits. But how has the mountain spirit's hall changed? The mountain spirit's hall is the space of this complex. The sun is now on the ceiling; it has gotten bright. On the altar is the spiny fish and *a fiery wheel*. Behind the altar it remains dark: that is the place of maternal shelter. We have already spoken of the illumination of this room. The situation has become "clear as day." The wheel of fire on the altar adds a further meaning. Wheels of fire were used at the time of the solstice as well as at Easter. When spring came, fire wheels were made and rolled over the fields and down the slopes. This was supposed to renew the sun's strength for another climb. Later this Germanic custom became a Christian Easter custom, since the same symbolism fit the newly born sun and the resurrected Christ. The wheel of fire is clearly another sign of spring, a sign that life has returned to its course, that winter, this psychic winter of being enclosed in the mountain, is over. There might also be a reference to the emotions here. A fiery wheel or a fiery horse means that the emotions are there and can once again be experienced in a certain orderly fashion.

The princess throws herself into the arms of the mountain spirit "as though in despair." This "as though," indicating uncertainty, is another example of the ambivalence we have already seen so much of. And now she is to think of the mountain spirit's head. "No mortal being could think of that," says the mountain spirit, "least of all a human." The mountain spirit puts his ultimate power at stake: his head, the seat of his thoughts, so distinguishes him that humans cannot even think of it. But this is not quite the case, for Peter knows his thoughts quite well, albeit with the help of his spirit companion. The mountain spirit really is no longer the sole possessor of his head, even before it is cut off. And when the princess asks for the riddle this time, her voice quavers, "as though *her* life or death depended on it." This is actually accurate, because if Peter guesses the riddle, she will regain her life, but if he does not, she will fall irrevocably into the clutches of the mountain spirit.

After she has regained her senses, she is given to Peter as his wife. Through Peter's action she had fainted and become powerless, and it is only after this event that she can regain her senses. She who had hitherto tyrannized the world around her through her withdrawn moods, outbreaks of rage, beheadings, and so on, is now *completely without power*. This shows that the power of the mountain spirit is broken. Peter wants to go see his companion immediately. The companion gives him one last piece of advice before departing. Once the mountain spirit has been eliminated, the dead man's spirit can also go.

So the princess is released from the mountain spirit and Peter from the dead man's spirit. Now at last the shadow problem mentioned earlier is resolved.

But what is this last piece of advice that the dead man's spirit gives Peter? He is to put a tub of water near the bed, and at night when the princess wants to go out, he is to submerge her in it until a raven emerges and then a dove. Only then will the right and proper princess be there again. This baptismal or immersion motif betokens the renewal that follows the drowning of the old.

So the princess still wants to go out at night, but this should be prevented. Obviously, more changes await her. The raven is often a symbol of the devil, or for evil altogether. Odin has on his shoulders the two ravens Hugin and Munin, although they stand for the creative principle, while Odin's wolf stands for the destructive principle. Nevertheless, this raven could symbolize a princess with dark, all-too-sinister thoughts. By contrast, the dove has been a symbol of peace from the time of the story of Noah's ark and the olive branch. In connection with a baptism, it reminds us of the dove of the Holy Spirit. In general, the dove evokes the qualities of peacefulness, purity, and gentleness. Psychologically, this harmonizes quite well with the fact that doves are very aggressive creatures, and this aggressivity is hidden behind a great show of delicacy and gentleness. For this reason, we should see through the princess's supposed tranquillity. And both behavior patterns are represented by birds, not people. They are thus not human, still not at all down-to-earth enough. By submerging the princess when each of these birds appear (in other words, rejecting her in these forms), she is brought finally to her human form. The angelic beauty and goodness she is then supposed to have sounds a bit oversweet. But angelic beauty and goodness need not exclude the possibility of her coming to terms with her aggression. All the same, we might well wish for the tale to continue so that the princess could become still more down-to-earth.

We have considered this fairy tale primarily in terms of masculine psychology. From this point of view it is a tale of a man breaking out of his attachment to his father, which always also means attachment to collective values and the societal order; and having broken out of this, he sees what this system lacks. He finds all those values that are poor and dead in himself, but which, when paid attention to, possess considerable power. So, on one side of this story is the spirit who is poor and dead and, on the other side, this repressed mountain spirit, who is aggressive and omnipotent in his destructiveness. The story brings the feminine side of Peter—which first has to be discovered because it was not present in the patriarchal framework out of which he came—under the influence of this mountain spirit. A condition of extreme psychological imbalance exists, particularly with regard to the aggressive emotions. And in looking at this feminine side, one has the very strong feeling that possession by the mountain spirit leads to a sadomasochistic behavior pattern. Having a feminine side that sets one riddles and beheads one when they are not guessed is a serious problem. This feminine side wants and does not want to be set free. It is trapped in a circling pattern, now suffering passively, now raging. It is impossible under these circumstances to lead a fruitful life. What is needed is to see the mountain spirit behind this and eliminate him. This, however, requires following one's feminine side on its excursions and watching critically but, at the same time, empathetically. Peter beating the princess with rods could mean that one does not merely tolerate these excursions but also beats the princess in oneself—in other words, is critical toward oneself. But to me it seems that the other point we made before is also important here, that Peter also intentionally takes on some of the aggression: not all of his aggression remains unconscious even if it only becomes conscious when focused on his own feminine side, that is, against himself. The key seems to be seeing the demon in oneself and decapitating it when the time comes, that is, reaching a point where one simply no longer allows oneself this destructiveness, this joy in torturing. But this is only possible after Peter has integrated a part of this mountain spirit, more or less the part of him that is most human.

The situation with the princess can also be understood from the point of view of feminine psychology. The princess is also under paternal domination, as has been shown in various ways.

This is in fact doubly so: she is under the domination of her own father, but also under that of the mountain spirit, a negative, demonically arrogant father. This does not mean that her own father also has to be demonic. Psychologically, it is even more probable that his aggression is inhibited, that he has also repressed the demonic aspect of his own being. The princess suffers the collective fate of being formed in the shadow of these fathers, especially by the sides of them that are repressed, because it is impossible to engage and work with those sides. In the absence of such attention, they simply impose themselves. At the beginning of our interpretation we said that Peter was seeking the collective shadow aspect; now we find that for the princess this takes the form of an extremely demonic father figure whose motto is "The more you suffer, the more others should suffer," the more you should take pleasure in others suffering at your hand. This could be called the sadomasochistic motto. The fairy tale describes the state in which the motto is fulfilled as an evil curse. This curse unfortunately is quite widespread. It is a vicious circle that contains no possibility of release within it.

This vicious circle brings suffering without transformation, because the suffering does not come from facing reality. It is the vicious circle of someone who has been deeply injured, someone who cannot confront the adversary on an equal footing. It is interesting that in the tale, the princess identifies the blows of the rod as hail. There is nothing one can do against hail, whereas there are definite measures one can take against being beaten with a rod. She is not capable of facing whatever is dealing out these blows. In psychological terms we speak of inhibited aggression. Aggression cannot be lived out overtly and is perverted into some other form, whether it results in highly destructive outbreaks or in misplaced aggression. Aggression is not aimed at its cause, but is played out in an area where one is less afraid of inflicting damage on oneself.

What is behind this circular pattern? In the fairy tale it is the bond with the mountain spirit, "spirit of the heights." This is a bond with a fascinatingly destructive side of the psyche; it is an identification with it. One meets this where all that is constructive has been negated out of the conviction that ultimately the situation is futile anyhow. It is fascinating, although it causes suffering, because identifying with it is an experience of power, as our fairy tale so excellently illustrates. This power experience is the antipodes of the very low self-esteem of someone who has been hurt. Those who suffer greatly often identify with the figure of Christ. The underlying idea is the hope of solving the problem of being unable to deal effectively with the world by identifying with either the Christ figure or an omnipotently evil figure, or both. But this form of salvation does not work. Though perhaps hoping for salvation, someone caught in such a circle is also very skeptical of it. Intense desire for it and rejection of this desire fight with each other. This ambivalence is understandable, for deliverance means losing the mountain-spirit refuge; with the loss of this, something wonderful in the feeling world would disappear from the life of this person—something wonderful, even if that means wonderfully destructive.

In our fairy tale the princess is saved. This takes place in two steps:

The first step makes possible the integration of the shadow that was so long repressed, and thereby Peter's acceptance of his own aggression, who stands for a new male generation. Looking at this now from the point of view of feminine psychology, we see that the masculine aspects of a woman must also accept this inherent aggression and self-assertiveness in order to renounce the motto, "the more I suffer, the more you have to suffer." This also lifts the ban on overt aggression, and reduces hidden aggression, which can be quite brutal.

The *second step* involves overcoming the mountain spirit and completing the baptism or immersion process.

If we relate this fairy tale to collective situations, we can see

that the fairy tale depicts a patriarchal society that strongly sup-
presses evil. The evil then manifests as the aggressive and destructive mountain spirit. So we have a very decent and proper society
with lots of laws that can be violated: propriety and decency with
a very aggressive, destructive undertone. This social situation has
a particular influence on women. Their conflict involves, on the
one hand, carrying out the role behavior demanded of them—in
the case of the princess, to be angelically beautiful and good, but
in so doing to be aggressively blocked in her masculine side—
and, on the other hand, having to become destructive, because
aggressivity cannot be reconciled with the accepted image; and
the woman, as the unimportant element in the patriarchal system,
is in any case not in a position to assert herself.

From the point of view of male psychology, what happens is
that the feminine aspect is undervalued and repressed and in this
way plays into the hands of repressed shadow. This, however,
means that a man's feminine aspects become endlessly irritable,
with angelic and diabolic states of mind alternating between each
other. This fairy tale shows the way out of these compulsive ruts.
The man must see his shadow, go along with it, trust it, and redeem it.

NOTES

1. "Märchen aus dem Harz," in *Deutsche Märchen seit Grimm* (Munich: Diederichs Verlag), pp. 144ff.
2. Besides parallels in fairy tales, there is also a parallel in the Old
   Testament apocrypha in the Book of Tobias in which Sarah has already killed seven men when Tobias comes to court her (Tob. 7:11).

VERENA KAST

Bluebeard

On the Problem of the Destructive Animus

By *means of wealth, prestige, and power, and despite their uneasy feelings, Bluebeard succeeds again and again in binding women to him and then he tries to kill them, like all their predecessors, when they discover his secret. The interpretation presented here detects a sadomasochistic pattern of relationship: a dominating, destructive man stands in relationship to a woman who identifies herself with his apparent power until she realizes that her femininity must inevitably be destroyed by this relationship. If this closed circle in the male-female relationship is to be opened up, the woman can no longer merely project the Bluebeard animus on actual men so as to be able to struggle with it there; it is important for her to deal with it also in herself. Bluebeard in a woman is her destructive animus. If she becomes conscious of this, she can free herself from his power.*

There was once a man who possessed beautiful houses in town and county, gold and silver table service, furniture and embroideries, and gilded coaches. But unfortunately this man had a blue beard. This made him so ugly and repulsive to look at that there was no woman and no girl who did not fly from him.

One of his neighbors, a lady of high degree, had two very beautiful daughters. Bluebeard asked for one of them for his wife and left it to the mother to decide which of the two she would give him. But neither wanted him. One pushed him off on the other, because neither could reconcile herself to marrying a man with a blue beard. Besides, they found it frightening that he had already married several women, and no one knew what had become of them.

In order to get to know them better, Bluebeard invited the sisters, along with their mother and three or four of their best girlfriends and a number of young people from the neighborhood, to come to one of his country houses. They spent eight entire days there, making excursions, hunting and fishing, and at dances and feasts where titles and honors were conferred. They never slept at all but passed the nights in diversions and games. At last it reached the point where the youngest sister no longer found the beard of the master of the house so blue and even found him worthy of all honors. As soon as they returned to the city, the wedding was celebrated.

When a month had passed, Bluebeard told his wife that he had a journey to make in the provinces on important business that would take at least six weeks and he hoped she would amuse herself well in his absence. She could invite her girlfriends to visit and go to the country with them if she so desired. She should serve the best from kitchen and cellar. "Here are the keys," he then said. "These are for the two big rooms where the furnishings are kept, these are for the gold and silver tableware that are not used every day, these are for the iron chests where my gold and silver is kept, these are for the coffers with my precious jewels, and this is the main key for all the rooms and apartments. And this little key here, this is the key to the small room at the end of the long corridor on the ground floor. You may open everything and go into every room, except for this small room. I strictly forbid you to enter it. Should you nevertheless do so, you will be the object of my most formidable wrath." She promised to obey all his orders. He embraced her, climbed into his coach, and departed on his journey.

The neighbor woman and her girlfriends did not wait to

be invited to visit the young married girl, for they were burning with curiosity to see all the riches of the house. So long as the husband had been there, they had not dared to come, because they were afraid of his blue beard. Now, however, they rushed through the rooms, through the bed-chambers and clothes closets, each one more splendid than the next. Then they climbed up to the rooms where the furnishings were kept, and there was no end to their amazement over the many magnificent carpets, beds, sofas, chests with secret compartments, tables, the mirrors in which one could see oneself from head to foot that had frames of glass, of silver, of gilded silver, the most beautiful and splendid they had ever seen. There was no end to their extravagant praise nor to their envy of their friend's good fortune. But the young woman took no real joy in seeing all these treasures, so impatient was she to open the little room on the ground floor.

She was so driven by curiosity that she gave no thought to the rudeness of leaving her guests to themselves. Down a small secret stairway she hurried with such great haste that she almost broke her neck two or three times. When she arrived at the door of the little room, she paused for a moment and thought about her husband's prohibition and considered that her disobedience might cause her unhappiness. But the temptation was so great that she yielded to it. She took the key and tremulously opened the door to the room.

At first she saw nothing because the window shutters were closed. After a few seconds she could make out that the floor was stained with blood. And in this blood was reflected the bodies of a number of female corpses that were fastened around the walls. The young woman thought she would die of fright, and the key, which she had taken out of the lock, fell from her hand. When she had come to her senses a bit, she picked up the key, locked the door again, and climbed up to her room in order to regain her composure. But this she did not succeed in doing; her agitation was too great.

Noticing that the key was flecked with blood, she wiped it two or three times, but the blood would not come off. Try as she might to wash it, and scrub it with sand and sandstone, the key remained bloody, for it was bewitched. There was no way to clean it; if she managed to get the blood off one side, it reappeared on the other.

On that very same evening, Bluebeard returned from his journey. He said that he had received letters en route saying that the business on account of which he had undertaken the journey had already been settled in his favor. His wife did everything in her power to show him how charmed she was over his early return. The next day he asked her to return his keys. She trembled so as she gave them to him that he had no trouble guessing what had occurred.

"How does it come about that the key to the little room is not among them?" he asked.

"I must have left it upstairs on my table," she replied.

"Don't forget to give it to me later," said Bluebeard.

She delayed as long as possible, but finally she had to bring him the key. When Bluebeard had examined it, he said to his wife: "Why is there blood on this key?"

"That I don't know," responded the poor woman, paler than death.

"That you don't know?" cried Bluebeard. "But I know! You had to go into the little room! Now, my love, you shall go in—and take your place next to the other ladies you saw there."

She threw herself sobbing at her husband's feet, begged for mercy, and showed genuine remorse at having been so disobedient. She was so beautiful and so desperate she would have softened a rock. But Bluebeard's heart was harder than a rock.

"You must die, my love, and indeed, at once!"

"If I must die," she answered, looking at him with her eyes streaming with tears, "give me a little time to pray to God."

"I'll give you half a quarter-hour," responded Bluebeard, "but not an instant longer."

Once upstairs in her room alone, she called to her sister, saying: "My dear Anne" (for that was her sister's name), "please climb up to the tower and see if our brothers are coming. They promised to visit me today. If you see them, give them a sign to hurry."

The sister climbed up to the tower and the poor desperate girl called to her from time to time: "Anne, my sister Anne, don't you see something coming?"

And the sister answered her: "I see only the sun shining and the grass growing green."

Then Bluebeard, with a big hunting knife in his hand, shouted with all his might to his wife: "Come down immediately, or I'm coming up!"

"Just another moment, please," his wife begged and called softly to her sister: "Anne, my sister Anne, don't you see something coming?" And the sister answered: "I see only the sun shining and the grass growing green."

"Come down now, immediately!" shouted Bluebeard.

"I'm coming," his wife replied and then called: "Anne, my sister Anne, don't you see something coming?"

"I see a big cloud of dust coming toward us," the sister replied.

"Is it our brothers?"

"Oh no, dear sister, it is a herd of sheep."

"Once and for all, will you come down?" Bluebeard roared.

"Just another second," replied his wife and then called: "Anne, my sister Anne, don't you see something coming?"

"I see two riders coming toward us," the sister answered, "but they are still far away!" And then right afterward: "Thanks and praise to God! It is our brothers! I'll give them a sign as best I can to get them to hurry."

Then Bluebeard shouted so loud that the whole house shook. The poor woman went down and threw herself at his feet, dissolved in tears, her hair all disheveled. "All that will do you no good," said Bluebeard. "You must die." With one hand, he took her by the hair and with the other he raised the hunting knife to cut off her head. The poor woman looked at him with deathly fear in her eyes and begged him to grant her a last moment so she could compose herself. "No, no," he said, "commend your soul to God." He raised his arm.

At that instant, there was such a loud knock at the door that Bluebeard paused briefly. The door opened and two cavaliers with swords in their hands dashed straight at Bluebeard. He recognized his wife's two brothers, the dragoon and the musketeer, and immediately took flight in order to save himself. But the two brothers were on his heels and caught him before he could reach the staircase. They ran him through with their swords and left him lying dead.

The poor woman was almost as dead as her husband. She no longer had the strength to stand up and embrace her brothers.

It turned out that Bluebeard had no heirs, and so all his wealth fell to his wife. She used a portion of it to marry off her sister Anne to a young nobleman whom she had long loved. With another part she acquired for her brothers the rank of captain, and the rest she brought as a dowry to her marriage with a very worthy man who made her forget the bad time she had spent with Bluebeard.[1]

There are many versions of "Bluebeard," but they all have in common that Bluebeard chops his wives up and always wants a new one. In some versions, as in ours, he is killed. In other versions, the heroine escapes from him, or escapes at least with her life. He is never transformed. Bluebeard is always portrayed as very rich, and always it is his possessions that cause the women to marry him in spite of the fact that they always find his blue beard frightening.

What is there about this blue beard?

According to Bolte and Polivka, in the sixteenth century a man whose black beard shone with bluish highlights was called a "*barbe bleue.*"[2] Such men were regarded as womanizers. Perrault saw in this blue beard something abnormal and eerie. Some fairy tales present a figure with a red or green beard. Some other odd feature can also appear in place of the blue beard. Thus Bluebeard appears in the Italian version as a bridegroom with a silver nose, and in a Finnish version as a bridegroom with a golden nose. In both the Italian and Finnish versions, Bluebeard eats corpses. From this Bolte and Polivka conclude that the Bluebeard figure might originally have been a god of death.

Presumably this tale is related to the ballads found throughout Europe that tell of the sex murderer who is killed by a maiden he has carried off into the woods, or by her brother (Bolte and Polivka). In our version, the forbidden room is a new component. We find it also in many other tales, for example, "Mary's Child" (Grimm's no. 3).

The story says that the blue beard makes the man so "ugly and repulsive" that all women fly from him. So this blue beard also makes people afraid of him. Since no one has a blue beard, this blueness characterizes him as somehow beyond what is normal and human. It is something extraordinary in both a positive and a negative sense. If Bluebeard had not wanted to demonstrate his extraordinariness, he could easily have shaved off this blue beard.

The story makes the blueness of his beard an expression of his future wife's alienation from him. Later she suddenly no longer finds the beard so blue, that is, she no longer finds the man so repulsive. This is not because his beard has somehow become less blue, but because she has become captivated by his wealth.

The fact that he seems to have a trade in women, even one with a high turnover, is no longer referred to. His wealth and power overcome all the justified feelings of uneasiness; material values replace eros, identification with someone else's property replaces one's own potential: in short, a marriage takes place.

Bluebeard does not wait long to put his wife to the test. Is she the obedient mate? Does he want to be sure that he is still the master of the household?

He lures his wife into disobeying him with a show of generosity. He confers on her the authority connected with the keys, while at the same time mentioning the room she may not enter. In this way, he more or less seduces her into entering this forbidden room, for this is where his secret is.

But what is Bluebeard's secret? Murdered women. We knew it from the beginning: Bluebeard is a consumer of women. Bluebeard is often envisaged as a corpse-devouring god of death. If he is a god of death, he is a god of death for women only.

So the secret is that he kills women, and indeed always at the point when they discover his secret. But obviously he wants them to discover his secret. Otherwise, why would he provide each woman with the little key?

As we have pointed out, every fairy tale can be interpreted on different levels. In one way, it can be interpreted as an expression of a typical individual psychological problem; in another, as a general problem of the times. These two are directly related.

Bluebeard is, on one hand, the representative of a patriarchal society that is in a state of war with women—or with the feminine principle altogether. Here relationships with women are based on blind obedience. He tests the women he is supposed to have relationships with and then kills them. However, he seems to make up for this quite well through his relationship with materiality. Materiality, material goods, after all, represent an aspect of the feminine principle (the *mater materia*), and though Bluebeard cannot have any genuine personal relationship, he can at least have wealth. Thus we have a situation depicted in which an enthrallment with materiality has become demonically acute. A real woman cannot survive alongside a demonic attachment to matter.

The tragedy is that the women, despite their justifiably uneasy feelings, play along with Bluebeard: they allow themselves to be dazzled by his wealth and the honor of being the wife of such a rich man; they even indulge their vanity by trying to dazzle their envious female friends.

It is important to see Bluebeard in his relationship to women, because by himself he is not a problematic figure. The essential problem is that, having been lured into his realm, the women are killed. But the women would not be killed if they did not go along with Bluebeard. Bluebeard never kidnaps the women; he merely seduces them. That is the difference between him and the so-called sex murderer.

In terms of the psychology of an individual, Bluebeard can be seen as an animus figure. From that point of view, the blue beard marks the animus as other-worldly—there is always a quality of unreality about him. It might be frightening or bewitching, but it is also always fascinating.

The color blue expresses something spiritual; but in this case it seems to me that "eerie" is perhaps a more accurate word. At the same time, his blue beard can be seen as an expression of his cold-bloodedness.

By means of riches, power, and role-playing, Bluebeard has once again caught himself a woman. If we take Bluebeard as an animus figure, this would mean that through fascination with these things and through drowning out one's uneasy feelings—one's own emotional reaction, which is undoubtedly present—an enthrallment with this animus is constellated that murders the feminine principle in oneself. In terms of the wife, this means that she gives up her own values in favor of Bluebeard's.

The extreme to which this is carried is shown by the fact that she is unable to tame her curiosity; she is urgently compelled to learn her husband's innermost secret. Let us imagine this for a moment in a real relationship. Wanting so urgently to penetrate into the innermost sphere of the other, not allowing the other any secrets, does not indicate a sense of close relationship; what it really indicates is possessiveness. This is confirmed by all the impatience: Bluebeard's wife runs down the secret staircase with such haste that she nearly breaks her neck two or three times.

This seems to me emblematic of the entire psychological situation. In a sense she has already broken her neck, or very nearly. In any case, there is need for a fundamental transformation. And, in this impatient seeking, we can see one form of obsession. The wife of Bluebeard as an image represents the desire to possess, however far this desire to possess might go.

However, she does not get to see what she wanted to see; instead she sees the murdered women. It is as though the room shows the cost at which the riches were accumulated: one's own missed or murdered potentialities. One cannot help thinking of the lot of so many women who have been totally assimilated into the lives of their husbands and have really become somewhat like children. They are unable to live out their own potentialities, which they have quietly and unobtrusively buried in some ground-level room. Bluebeard was too fascinating.

And now the young woman believes she is going to die of fright—and the key falls from her hand, the key that is the living witness of her disobedience. She can no longer deny what she has seen. There is no longer any possibility of denial; she has passed the point of no return. She must acknowledge her deed. She is terrified. Being terrified about something is not a terribly gentle form of consciousness expansion. Here it is a case of being gripped by panic. All the feelings that were hitherto repressed now seem to break through with concentrated force.

This fright is ongoing: the key can no longer be cleansed of blood; the relationship with Bluebeard is disrupted. Now she knows about this horrible side of Bluebeard's wealth and power. And that is not all. She also knows that he wanted to hide that side. Thus it is only logical that he will kill her too.

Once more, this can be seen on two levels: the personal and

the collective. On the collective level, in a society where power and tyranny are the dominant values, if a few people "see the corpses" that have been hidden away, those people have to be eliminated for the sake of the system. This is a very common mechanism and it is not by any means reserved for women. It is easier to call somebody an idiot than to really open the last room, admit the errors of the system, and take responsibility for making changes.

This mechanism can also be seen to function in the women's liberation movement. Women who see that they are unable to realize their potential (that they themselves play a part in this is something they recognize somewhat less often) lay the blame in a way that hurts men. And men, as is usual when something hurts too much, react irascibly and strike back.

On the more personal level, what we have is a woman who suddenly realizes that although she does share in the power and authority, something in her is not participating, and that her own life is clearly hanging by a single thread.

Here the sudden fear of not having really lived and not really being able to live what is essential to her seems to be quite on the mark. Her shock is over the fact that so much of her cannot live within this constellation where she thought everything was so ideal, as well as her realization that she herself is in some way Bluebeard—in other words, somehow very brutal herself. What the woman also encounters in this forbidden room is death. This is true in our version of the tale as well as in those versions in which she sees her husband eating corpses. These phenomena have to be seen together. It is not just death but murder, violent death, that we feel did not have to happen, therefore it seems even more brutal. She becomes conscious of death and in doing so, she "thought she would die of fright."

What is the significance of becoming conscious of death? We are talking here about becoming conscious, not coping. This nevertheless means seeing death as a possibility that has hitherto been excluded—especially in the midst of the flashy lifestyle embodied by Bluebeard—and to see it as a possibility for *oneself*. It is a peculiar feeling when one realizes—not intellectually but existentially—that at some point one is going to die. Only when this has happened does it become possible to immerse oneself fully into the eternal ebb and flow of life as a whole, not merely to experience the pain that is part of all passing away, but also to sense the meaningfulness of it, to feel there is space for the fresh and new. At the same time the value of being here and of things being as they are here and now is infinitely increased. In the face of change, life places much greater value on the here and now. Life itself acquires that unique quality that we so often think we have to manufacture.

In his essay on authority, Wilke writes that it is only possible to solve the problem of authority when one is confronted with the problem of death.[3] I would like to take that further: this not only applies to the authority problem as a specific form of the problem of power, but to the problem of power in general. The exercise of power can be seen as a desperate attempt to evade, in the broadest sense, the necessity of dying. In this way the lust for power appears as an attitude of avoidance. The exercise of power can often be seen as an attempt to gain power over death. Death can be understood as a very profound change, a change from which no one knows how he or she will emerge. The attitude of power is to stubbornly hold onto its conscious position and thus, so to speak, enforce the status quo. But then it is also important to build up power on the concrete level so as to have something to oppose to death. This is expressed in our fairy tale in which it becomes necessary to outwit death.

A further example, and there are many others, is the French fairy tale "How Death Was Made a Fool." In this story, a kindly old woman prevails upon a saint to grant her the power to cast a spell that forces people up the tree in front of her house. She casts the spell on Death as well. After a few years, with nobody dying in the world and the distress resulting from this becoming so great, she begins to feel sorry for those who have to suffer so much without being able to die, and she lets Death come down from the tree. But first she makes him promise to spare her for a few years.

In the tale "The King's Son and Death," the king's son stays in the forest with Death for three years and Death teaches him secret knowledge. Death tells him that if he sees Death at the head of a sick bed, then the patient belongs to him (Death), but if Death is sitting at the foot of the bed, then the king's son, as the doctor, will be able to cure him. After a hundred years, the king's son, who of course in the meantime has become king, grows old and weak and sees his master sitting at the head of the bed. He asks to be spared long enough to say the Lord's Prayer, a request Death gladly grants. But he recites only the first half of the prayer. He waits a hundred years to say the second half and by then he has nothing against dying.

When we realize on an existential level that we have to die, we momentarily have feelings that are illuminating, clear, and transparent. These feelings show us life in a new, broader perspective. At that point, power becomes something totally futile. Faced with another person's death, we experience a similar shift in our sense of life. The experience of death always separates the divine from the supposedly divine and thus once again opens us up to that divine quality which broadens our circumference. By contrast, power makes us narrow and destructive.

Once a woman realizes how dangerous it is to commit herself to Bluebeard, her fascination with him is lost—not least because he is relativized by death. Then comes the phase of defending oneself against him. There now takes place in the woman a complete rejection of everything Bluebeard stands for, be it authority, power, or aggression—if we needed a catchword, we might call it general possessiveness. None of these qualities are inherently bad. But when they manifest themselves *exclusively*, no longer permitting other sides to be lived, whether these are other sides of one's own personality, other people, other feelings, or other views, then they become mortally dangerous. Bluebeard is perhaps more often at work than is generally thought.

The confrontation with Bluebeard consists of the woman no longer being involved with Bluebeard but rather consciously allying herself with everything that he doesn't stand for. In her mortal fear, she pretends to want to pray. She does not, however, do this, not at least in this version of the tale. All the same, this is interesting as an intention or an idea, and meaningful as a possibility of concentrating on a more all-embracing divinity. In a French parallel version of this tale, there is a little grayhaired man called Father Jacques to whom the wife rushes for protection. Again in other versions—such as the Spanish "Girl without Arms," the middle part of which contains a very clear Bluebeard parallel in which Bluebeard is the devil—the girl calls upon the pure Virgin Mary for help.

In all the versions in which the woman turns to a power opposed to Bluebeard and more all-embracing than he is, Bluebeard is conquered and eliminated. In the other versions, in which the woman outwits Bluebeard on her own, he is sometimes burned but sometimes he simply goes back to his house where he presumably waits for his next victim.

If we see Bluebeard as an animus figure—one who embodies a typical transpersonal experience—then only a superior spiritual principle can provide a remedy against him. For the animus in whatever form is always something that fascinates us. And that which has this fascinating quality always leads us to spirituality.

In our tale, the woman calls to her sister, who is supposed to tell her if her brothers are coming. Thus she turns to a side of herself that is not under Bluebeard's spell: "I see only the sun shining and the grass growing green." This statement throws some light on the sister. Even in this situation, she still sees the sun shining and the grass growing green—she still sees life. This is a great contrast to the death chamber below on the ground floor. This sister, however, is the intermediary for the wife's two swashbuckling brothers. In the image of the sun shining and the grass growing green, we have an enormous contrast to Bluebeard sharpening his knife below and to the tense atmosphere altogether. One must contemplate these images inwardly to appreciate the consoling counterpoise they provide. (Here the meditative approach to fairy tales suggests itself.) The grass can grow even while Bluebeard threatens. It is a wonderful image of continuous growth, of letting things take their course until the brothers arrive. There is also again a strong sense of distancing oneself, of remaining uninvolved—even at the point where there is almost no way out anymore. And just as Bluebeard is about to lose patience entirely, a cloud of dust appears—but it is a herd of sheep and not the brothers.

We can of course take the point of view that the narrator devised this herd of sheep in order to heighten the suspense, but even so the image is quite well chosen. Sheep are dependent on a bellwether, which they follow uncritically. And since the bellwether itself is not necessarily very intelligent, we have the strange phenomenon of herds of sheep charging about without direction, even into abysses if abysses happen to be there. In this symbol, the authority-related dependency on Bluebeard as a mortally dangerous inhibition is represented and given a value. Nonetheless, the herd of sheep is there primarily to indicate the complete hopelessness of the situation. Distancing oneself now is no help; even this kind of defense must some time or other lose its effectiveness. Something new has to enter the picture: the brothers.

The brothers are swashbuckling companions, a dragoon and a musketeer. They run Bluebeard through before he can reach the staircase. Brothers are often animus figures who are very close to consciousness. They are not at all like Bluebeard; they are energetic comrades who represent here a very resolute kind of action—the elimination of the Bluebeard situation.

But before this solution could occur, it was important to fully experience the tension in the image of Bluebeard sharpening his knife and the helpless wife who has finally recognized his hideousness.

By the end the poor wife is nearly as dead as her husband. This shows what she has been through, but it is also an indication of a transformation: If Bluebeard is no longer her husband, then she is a new person, someone much more closely identified with herself. As a proper consequence of this, the riches fall to her. She divides these very justly among her siblings. This sounds so logical and matter of fact, but it is not if we consider how up till now all Bluebeard's riches have been hoarded. The brothers are raised in status. They become captains, in other words, leading figures.

We can interpret this second part of the fairy tale on a more collective level. In a situation dominated by power and aggression, the first step is to realize what is being murdered and to be frightened by it. This kind of a patriarchal situation can be maintained by women as well as by men—in essence this has nothing to do with men as opposed to women.

Distancing oneself is the next step. One does this in the knowledge that it is simply "inflated" to fight things that go far beyond one's powers, where there is little doubt who in the long run will be the stronger party. This means distancing oneself but at the same time realizing that one is in the danger zone. Next, one must mobilize all available forces that do not belong to Bluebeard's sphere. A solution cannot be forced, it must be eked out. For women in this situation, the idea would be to seek solidarity with their sisters. This leads to a reinforcement of self-esteem once the Bluebeard-related elements of jealousy and power struggle have disappeared. On the basis of this reinforcement, indeed in direct connection with it, active self-defense develops.

On the whole then, this fairy tale is about how to free oneself from an extreme situation of domination and destructiveness. And this situation can be found both inwardly and outwardly—each presumably affecting the other.

But in this story a particular pattern of relationship is also presented. We have a domineering, aggressive, destructive man and a woman who identifies with his strength, but then becomes aware that she herself is no longer really living. This is a pattern of relationship that is nowadays very heavily under fire. But it is a relationship *pattern*, and that means that it is not only the man who is to blame for it. Precisely in this kind of situation, a Bluebeard animus is often projected onto the man. In this projection the woman fights and defeats herself. It seems important for the woman's movement that women experience Bluebeard not only as a projection, but as a part of themselves as well—someone they must deal with in themselves, if he is there.

Once again, we have a sadomasochistic context, but this fairy tale seems to go at this problem much more from the point of view of feminine psychology. I think we should see the sadomasochistic problem in broad terms the way Schorsch and Becker do in their book *Angst, Lust, Zerstörung*.[4]

The essential point here is domination of the other, total power over the other. The other is dominated and submits. These roles are interchangeable or can persist onesidedly. As soon as a society is split up into inferior and superior people, the way is open for sadistic practices. We are acquainted with this from the Inquisition, war, torture, and so on.

Though it is covered up in our society, there is a whole sector that functions in accordance with the Bluebeard pattern of power and impotence. We have only to think of schools, orphanages, prisons, and to some extent, families.

It is always interesting in this context how much interest the "real sadists," for example, sex murderers, arouse in the entire population. Here projection has a field day; one's own sadistic tendencies can be lived out in fantasy.

Incidentally, Schorsch and Becker show in their book that for the sex murderer, pleasure is hardly the point. Rather, the criminal act is an expression of the collapse of his defenses. The primary part of his defense was to shift sadism onto sexuality, so that outside of this realm he could still function normally.

In this fairy tale and in the previous one, "The Cursed Princess," but quite clearly in reality as well, the circular behavior pattern of sadomasochism makes relationship to a great extent impossible. On one hand, one would like to fuse with one's partner, but at the same time one would like to remain detached.

Schorsch and Becker definitely regard sadomasochism as a partnership problem. However, it can also be seen in the relationship that we have with ourselves, that is, on the subjective level. It appears in all forms of suppressing and being suppressed.

As a partnership problem, as already indicated, it goes something like this: One partner feels and behaves like the strong one; the other feels and behaves as the weak one and identifies with the strength of the partner, much in the same way a child identifies with the strength of his father. In this way he himself becomes weaker and weaker and can simply surrender, or he can also begin to defend himself—indirectly, through the power tactics of the weak (such as sickness), or, ultimately, directly as well. This is a relationship pattern that we often encounter when someone is trying to "save" someone else. The problem with such a relationship is that the weakness of the dominant party and the strength of the subordinate one are both projected onto the other. Both are then lacking something that should be part of their own personalities. Thus the resolution of such a relational pattern can only take place through one party seeing and accepting his strength and the other seeing and accepting his weakness. Obvious examples of this pattern leap easily to mind. But in every relationship there are quite subtle sadomasochistic patterns—for example, in an analytic relationship in which one of the parties tends to play the victim. When one party plays the victim, the role of dominator or sadist is immediately delegated. The other is made into something evil, and from that the victim derives the right and obligation to defend himself.

What is the point of this roundabout approach? It is quite simple: one finagles for oneself the right to be aggressive without having to take responsibility for it—after all, one is only defending oneself! At the same time one builds up authority as an objective where it is not necessary at all. We want authority, but at the same time we do not want it. This ambivalence is a vestige of the transitional period when we still needed a mother and father but at the same time wanted to be independent. The problem with remaining stuck in the ambivalence of that phase is that one ends up cutting one's own potentialities to pieces.

NOTES

1. Perrault, *Märchen aus alter Zeit* (Melzer Verlag, 1976).
2. J. Bolte and G. Polivka, *Anmerkungen zu den Kinder- und Hausmärchen der Brüder Grimm*, vol. 1 (Hildesheim: Olms,1963), p. 409.
3. H.-J. Wilke, "Autoritätskomplex und autoritäre Persönlichkeitsstruktur," in *Zeitschrift für Analytische Psychologie*, no. 8 (1977): 33–40.
4. E. Schorsch and N. Becker, *Angst, Lust, Zerstörung* (Hamburg, 1977).

VERENA KAST

THE GREEN MAIDEN

The Archetype of the Feminine in Upheaval

This fairy tale takes us deeper into the factors that lie behind a certain type of bewitchment of the male-female relationship that renders it unfruitful. There is a need for a fundamental transformation of our attitude toward Mother Nature, which in our culture has been repressed and driven into the negative demonic sphere. Such a transformation would bring about new developments in both the masculine and feminine realms, as our fairy tale shows in an exemplary fashion. When something happens in a fairy tale in the realm of great archetypal figures such as the Green Maiden, it is always something that relates to both men and women. Nonetheless, this fairy tale is told primarily from the feminine perspective.

An old grandmother told this story and what she recounted was true. Here is what she said:

Now, listen to what I have to tell you. The story of the green maiden has just come to my mind. That's one you haven't heard yet. Yes, a lot happened in the old days, all of which would be forgotten if people like me didn't remember it and pass it along. Many years ago, down there in Windhausen among the wattle huts, there lived a poor broommaker who had many handsome children. That's a good thing when poor people have handsome children. This broommaker took his eldest daughter—she was a girl of thirteen or fourteen, who had red cheeks and bright shining eyes, and on top of that could talk like a book—anyway, the father took her along into the forest to gather birch brush for brooms, do you understand? At that time near Windhausen there were a lot of birch trees growing, and, you know, it's the fine birch rods that brooms are made from. It was terribly cold, even though the sun shone over hill and valley. The twigs were coated with ice, and they looked like sticks of pure silver hanging down from the trees. They went deeper into the forest. There used to be pines in that part of the forest, then later the hardwoods grew in. All of a sudden the father stopped incredulous in his tracks, and pointed toward a big pine, he said: "Look there, Anna, what in the world is that?"

The girl too saw a maiden standing there. She was wearing a green dress, had green hands, a green face, and even green hair. The two were still standing there amazed when the green maiden approached them and said to the father: "Your daughter there, her I must have." She had hardly said this before she vanished with the girl.

The man was so frightened that at first he couldn't budge from the spot. Then he came to himself again and heard a faraway cry: "August, August, August!" Then a few paces from him stood a golden stag. Thinking that his daughter had been transformed into the stag, he went toward it. But as he tried to grab the stag by its antlers so he could hold onto it, it vanished. This happened three times, each time in a different place.

In this way the broommaker came upon a little hut. He went inside to rest a bit from his efforts and from his worry over his daughter whom he had lost in such a terrible way. Lo and behold, there sat the green maiden, who was half fish and half human. Around her on little steps sat all kinds of little men with stone limbs, and not far away from the door sat the stolen girl, the broommaker's daughter, on a golden throne. Full of joy, the happy father took his child by the arm and made for home. No one followed him, and he ran like his hair was on fire until he got out of the forest and happily home to his family. But if the girl had been beautiful before, now she was a veritable angel of beauty.

Now the story got around, and it became known that the broommaker had a very beautiful daughter; why, she was so beautiful that even the youthful king came to hear of it! Since he had promised himself that he would marry only the best and most beautiful girl, he became acquainted with her and took her as his wife. That she was a mere broommaker's daughter was of no matter—he loved her, and she loved him a great deal indeed. Now that was a wonderful marriage. One could not have lived without the other. Whenever they met, they had to embrace and kiss, and oh, in a way that was so sincere, so heartfelt, so tender, and so loving that finally everybody said: "There is nobody as happy as our royal couple."

In this way a year passed in joy and pleasure. Then the young queen gave birth to a prince with three golden curls. This brought new rejoicing, great joy, and more heartfelt love. But nothing is perfect. During the first night after the birth, the green maiden appeared and spoke to the new mother: "Child, did you see me in my distress?" The queen replied: "My dearest mother, I didn't see you." Then the green maiden took the adorable prince, hugged him and kissed him and disappeared with him.

The whole land mourned for this loss, and the father and mother were nearly beside themselves with sorrow. But after a year, the queen gave birth to another darling prince, this one with a golden star on its breast. Now everyone was happy and content once more. But this didn't last long. Again, the first night after the birth, the green maiden appeared and said: "Child, did you see me in my distress?" The queen replied: "Dearest mother, I did not see you." Thereupon the green maiden once again disappeared with the child.

Once again there was sorrow, and the queen was almost

ready to do away with herself. After that, another year passed, and she had a third son, this one with a golden stag on its breast. Already several days beforehand, guards had been posted. The whole castle was surrounded by soldiers and before the door of the queen's room distinguished gentlemen were on guard, I don't know if they were chamberlains or not. In short, everything was done to keep the child from being stolen again. Nevertheless, at eleven o'clock on the first night, all the guards were lying fast alseep. Once again the green maiden came to the queen and spoke to her. "Child, did you see me in my distress?" And the new mother replied: "Dearest mother, I did not see you." Thereupon the green maiden disappeared with the child.

Since all measures had failed, the whole populace demanded that the queen be burned. She must have devoured her children, for they could not have been stolen; and then had the queen not had blood in her bed and on her hands and mouth each time on the morning after? The king did what he could not to give in, because he loved her too much. But at last he had to yield to what he was unable to change; otherwise the people would have killed him as well.

Now a great pyre was built, and the unfortunate mother was brought to it and tied to a stake. The minister prayed for her poor soul and asked dear God to accept her and take her to him. Then he blessed her and climbed down. Around the wood heap the people thronged, waiting to see the witch set afire. The musicians played gruesome music, and all began to wait for the moment when the wood would be ignited and the queen's torment would begin. At that instant, the green maiden appeared before her once again on the pyre and spoke: "Child, did you see me in my distress?" The queen said: "Dearest mother, I did not see you."

During this time, the executioner had been struggling to light the pyre, which did not seem to want to catch fire. Then the green maiden said: "Because you have been so discreet and silent, and even the prospect of hideous death at the stake has not brought you to tell all, you and I and your husband, the golden stag, are saved. Here are your children back." And there in an instant stood the three darling children next to the bound queen, embracing her knees and calling: "Mother, dear mother, where is our good father?" Then she put her arms around her children. The people were at first mute and motionless with amazement, but then they dragged everyone down from the pyre and brought them in jubilation to the astonished father while the musicians played joyful music. And so ends our story.[1]

The initial situation of the fairy tale shows a broommaker who is poor but has quiet handsome children. In comparison to other fairy tales like the Danube Valley tale "The Black Woman,"[2] here we do not have a situation of pronounced need. We have a situation where, though there is poverty, richness is also present in its midst.

At the beginning we have the broommaker and his daughter. At the end we have a green maiden, the girl, and a king in the form of a stag, all of whom have been redeemed, and three children as well. Thus, as we will see, it is not merely a completion that takes place but a substantial development.

This is a development in which the girl, as the protagonist, matures and finds a new identity. In addition, the masculine element emerges from a bewitchment and takes on human form. And then we have the addition of the three boys, who carry the masculine principle into a new generation.

The primary focus of the development, however, is the transformation that takes place in the realm of Mother Nature, or whatever we might like to call this green woman. This in turn leads to a change in the feminine *and* the masculine elements. It is always that way in fairy tales: when something happens that concerns truly major archetypal figures, it always relates to both men and women.

Thus a whole new attitude toward nature develops, allowing relationships to change. Men as well as women are freed from a certain rigidity and immobility, from a bewitchment, which, though it may be as golden as the stag is in this fairy tale, nevertheless remains a bewitchment.

Now that we have described the grand scheme and general meaning of the fairy tale, let us turn to its individual sequences.

To begin with, we have a broommaker, someone with a natural relationship to the forest, from which he gathers brushwood. He also has children, that is, life is perpetuated through him. No woman is mentioned; if there is one, then she is obviously not important here.

To gather birch brush[3] in the forest is to use it as an enlivening force; it can be used to make things clean, not very clean, but clean all the same. The attitude behind this is that one can make some use of the forest—symbolically understood as the realm of the unconscious—even if this amounts only to using the brushwood that one gathers. Something is being done with the unconscious, the unconscious is being made use of, even if only to a very small degree.

In the forest it is crisp and cold. Everything suggests frozenness, immobility. This immobility does not seem necessarily to come from consciousness. It simply seems to be the state of the winter forest. But at the same time the unconscious produces the antithesis of this crisp frigidity: the *green* maiden. Crisp cold on the one hand; the green maiden—more than green—on the other. The whole principle of greenness has obviously been intensified in this maiden. Green is the color of nature, of spring and the development that can wait until its time has come. The green maiden, however, is wholly a figure from a transcendental realm, a "goddess." A further characteristic of hers is indicated by the fact that the girl calls her "Mother." Thus she is a mother goddess. As is appropriate when encountering such a figure, the father and daughter are struck with awe.

Here the father does not, as in many parallel versions, bargain his daughter away. He just lets her be stolen. The father in this story has a relationship with his daughter, as can be seen from the fact that he takes her along into the forest. Clearly there is a father-daughter bond here. Beyond this, the father also has a relationship to the forest, to the unconscious—not a particularly profound relationship, but a relationship all the same—in a situation where the unconscious on the whole is immobilized. On account of this, the unconscious also becomes fascinating for the daughter who has the paternal bond. It is the father who leads her into its domain.

This is happening at an age when she is becoming an adult, ripening into womanhood. From this point of view, it is possible to see the fairy tale as a tale of a woman's maturation, but under the special conditions that prevail when maturation takes place in the cold at the beginning of winter. This is by no means usual— we would not ordinarily conceive of this state of childhood not yet quite awakened to womanhood as "cold." We will see also in connection with other passages that though this tale can be interpreted as being concerned with growing up, certain phenomena are not adequately explained by this interpretation. So if we take it as a tale of growing up, we must do so in a special sense. Puberty in itself has no particular significance—it is happening all the time. However, in relation to the attitude of the times and to the configuration of personal issues, it can have a special significance.

Fairy tales concerning growing up can also be understood in another way—as concerning the maturation of an entire generation rather than that of a single individual. Looked at in that way, what we really have is a tale of evolution with the goal of finding a new identity that is in harmony with a newly constellated archetype. Here the heroine embodies a collective event, thus becoming a collective necessity: "Your daughter there, her I must have."

As already mentioned, the unconscious is characterized here as immobile; it needs to be brought to life. This creates the condition necessary for people to be attracted by a new archetype. This happens not only because we need it, but also because *it* needs us.

The girl is taken away, and in her place is a golden stag. At first the father thinks his daughter is hidden in this stag. Here again he shows himself to be a person who knows something of the laws of the unconscious. For example, we recall from mythology a hind, or female deer, with golden antlers. It was the third labor of Hercules to bring this hind back alive to Mycenae. Hinds had no antlers in those days either, or if they did have them—and gold ones to boot—then they were divine beings. Artemis's companion was loved by Zeus and was therefore changed into a hind. In this myth, she *fled*, and because the hunter wanted to carry off this special quarry, she fled beyond the known hunting territory into another land, from which there was no return. Hercules pursued her for a year, then met Artemis, who was angry that he had caught the hind.

Stags in fairy tales have the primary task of luring mortals into a realm beyond. This is what happens in the fairy tale "The Two Brothers" (Grimm's no. 60). The stag is *fascinating* and cannot be captured. He can be compared to fascinating ideas, feelings, intuitions that one cannot really grasp but that nevertheless ultimately lead to a complex.

This stag already conveys the sense of something very essential, not least because it is golden. But it is shifty, at once a seducer and guide. Thus it leads the father to the house of the green maiden. This is, by the way, the only fairy tale of this type in which the father continues to concern himself with his daughter after she has been lost.

In the little hut, in which the father really only wanted to rest a bit from his efforts and worries, sits the green maiden. So he is not required to open a forbidden door. On the contrary, the green maiden, and especially the stag, have obviously set things up so he will find her. The stag definitely belongs to the domain of the green maiden. The impulse toward change in this fairy tale very clearly proceeds from the unconscious.

Inside the house is the green maiden, who is described as *half fish and half human*. It strikes one as peculiar in comparison with other similar fairy tales that this green maiden is not seeking a man, as water-nymphs or nixies typically do. The green maiden is different. She wants the young daughter.

This indicates another form of transformation: the liberation of the nixie. When a nixie is liberated by a man, then she remains to some extent bound to the water element. Thus in many tales, she must always be free on a Friday or Saturday, so that she can return to the water. She usually has certain conditions for marriage: that the man not spy on her, never hit her, and never abuse her verbally. Usually the man breaks his promise, and then she must return forever to the water. Often, however, she leaves children behind.

Thus it seems to me critical here that the green maiden says she needs the girl.

On closer examination, it becomes clear why she needs the girl. She has no legs. She lacks the ability to move over the earth; she is only able to move in water. This means that she must ever and again sink too deep into the unconscious; in other words, she is not sufficiently able to embody herself in consciousness. This fits with the fact that she is a *maiden* and thus has no children, which in consideration of the fish tail is no surprise. Symbolically, this points to her inability to have her own children, to be creative, that is, to make the unconscious conscious. This is also indicated by the little men with stone limbs sitting on little steps. Dwarfs in the realm of the Great Mother are usually creative, as we find, for example, in the following myth:

Rhea wants to give birth to Zeus. She is alone. She falls to the ground. The mountain produces as many spirits to help her with the birth as she has fingers. These helpers were later called Daktyloi. "In all these stories," Karl Kerényi notes, "the Daktyloi were servants and instruments of the Great Mother, obstetricians, smiths, and magicians, who may also be described, by reason of their seemingly small stature, as craftsmen-dwarfs."[4]

Since the little men in our tale have stone legs, they cannot move about; here, too, the creative aspect is petrified, immobile, a parallel to the frozen forest. Thus we see that the creative aspect of this mother imago is in a sorry state—this archetype is insufficiently able to manifest itself in life. This means, in terms of the collective, that life has become too uncreative, especially the life of women. If we look at this in terms of the personal psychology of the girl, we see that, though the possibility of her being a mother does exist—she is fourteen years old—it is not yet there in a completely actualizable form.

Now the broommaker's daughter is sitting not too far from the door on a golden throne. Normally, it is queens who sit on golden thrones. The girl is in a highly preferential position, and through the golden throne she is brought into relation with the golden stag. This could mean that in the whole story, which concerns matters that go far beyond the sphere of personal consciousness, she is assuming the primary position.

But the father takes her by the arm and immediately leads her away. He takes her to himself. In taking the big girl by the arm as if she were a child, the father indicates that he is not yet ready to surrender the daughter to her destiny. On the collective level, this is an indication that women are not yet able to pursue their own course.

But what does this whole situation mean from the perspective of the broommaker's daughter? She is captivated in the truest sense of the word by an archetype—the archetype of the green maiden. We have already seen that captivation is an aspect of the nature mother. Since the girl is thirteen or fourteen years old, we can imagine how it might be possible for her to get sudden glimpses of what it might be like to be a woman, a mother.

It is more probable, however, that she is simply inflated with the realm of fantasy—she sees herself as a queen in the land of the green woman, in the land of womanhood, which is primarily concerned with birth and development. Maybe she senses that somehow something is amiss with this process of birth and development.

All the same, she appears as a queen, even if only for a moment—the whole thing must have been like a dream for her—for the father immediately takes her away again, makes her into a little child again, brings her back to her old reality. This sequence beautifully expresses the function of the father-daughter bond, which is at once protective and inhibitory. While she abandons herself to the fascination of the unconscious, the father remains aware of its dangers, for her as well as for himself in his father role. This is why he makes her into a little child again. Nevertheless, through her fantasy she must have gained an impression of the greatness of being a woman—as well as a glimpse of the serious obstacles in the way of her attaining womanhood. She has received an insight into the underpinnings of her life in both its greatness and its limitations. Even if her father takes her away again, she already belongs to this realm and she will continue to belong to it. It will remain constellated until the stone limbs and the fish tail have disappeared.

The girl is now more beautiful than ever before. After having been carried off to the green maiden, she is more mature and therefore has also become more beautiful. The broommaker's daughter has confronted the great Mother Nature within herself and experienced, if only in an intuitive flash, that she has business in this realm, that she must make room in her life for this goddess. Perhaps just this intuition that something eternal is seeking to manifest through her and is essentially dependent upon her, is enough to bring about inner change—and give her a certain "golden" radiance.

No wandering in the forest follows this experience, as is the way in other fairy tales. The development seems to be broken off. The young king learns of her and marries her. The two love each other very much. But the young woman is not just beautiful, she is captivated by the green maiden, she is identified with her and her world.

What is the meaning of this? In the green maiden's little hut, male and female are together. We know from the end of the story that the stag is a bewitched man, and we also have the parallel of the little men with the stone legs. We can presume that the broommaker's daughter will project this entire world, complete with its nondifferentiation of male and female. And onto what or who else would she project it than onto her husband? As strange as it might sound, this means in actuality that her husband must also be a green maiden for her. In the story her husband is well suited to take on this projection, since he too belongs to the realm of the green maiden. As the golden stag he remains to be liberated from this archetypal domain. Here again we see that when matters relating to the essence of life are highlighted, both sexes are always concerned.

Such a transference onto the husband is something we encounter quite frequently in relationships in which one partner or both partners are inadequately disengaged from the mother archetype. In these cases, what is sought after—I am speaking now from the point of view of the woman—is for the partner to be both husband and mother at the same time. In concrete situations, this leads to immensely exaggerated demands on the husband, especially when liberation from the mother and the development of the consciousness of womanhood have both been rerouted through the husband, in other words, when the mother has to be fought in him.

This can of course all be formulated from the male side as well. Seen from that point of view, the man has to combat not only his mother—that is nothing unexpected—but also his father as projected on the woman. This provides an explanation for the allergic reaction men have to the animus.

The fairy tale itself speaks from the point of view of the woman who has to deal with this situation. Therefore we will also keep to this perspective. Just after the grandmother-narrator has once again stressed how much the broommaker's daughter and the prince love each other, she says: "But nothing is perfect." This points to the fact that this love, which is obviously based essentially on the ability of both partners to project the entirety of the "green-maiden world" on the other, though very beautiful, is not in the long run something that can stand up to the test of life.

Now the broommaker's daughter brings children into the world, which quite clearly proves her relationship to the realm of the green maiden. It is as though these children allow at least the male aspect of the green maiden, the golden stag, to become incarnated, born into the real world. Captivation by the unconscious (represented by the animal form) *seems* to be eliminated.

Up until now, we have developed our interpretation as though the king were a real man. He may well have been intended as such, but it seems to me that we really have to consider this entire situation on the subjective level.

It is typical of puberty that the archetypes of the feminine and the masculine remain to a great extent undifferentiated from each other. For this reason, persons in puberty often have a marked androgynous quality and can also behave in a bisexual manner. It is out of this that the girl's animus begins to crystallize and develop—animus in the broadest, rather than the pejorative sense. On a quite practical level, we see this in the need girls have to really get to know men, but it is no less visible in the interest that they take in intellectual and community matters. It is also to be seen in the powerful, eruptive longing for a meaning that first appears in this phase of development, in the fascination with the search for meaning, and in the enormous despair that occurs when no meaning appears. The lingering attachment of the animus to the Great Mother has the effect that everything remains somewhat excessive. In our fairy tale, where the Great Mother appears as a green maiden with a fish tail, great emphasis is placed on birth and development, natural growth, which at the same time entails an obstruction. Here the crux of the matter is to enable the green maiden, who with her fishtail still belongs to the "blue sphere" of water, to move into the "green sphere" of vegetation. The tale also focuses our attention on bringing the unconscious into life and the importance of the feminine and nature, including all the difficulty involved in dealing with these factors properly (we have only to think of the initial situation with the frozen forest). An entirely different accent would have been present had a "lady of the beasts" appeared in the story.

In relation to green, we of course also think of unripeness, as in green fruit. In this connection, there are interesting parallels to the green maiden, for example the figure of the green war god of the Aztecs, Xipetotec, who turns into the sun god Huitzilopochtli, who is also a war god. The sun god is a central god. Also, in Egyptian mythology, the green Osiris turns into the golden sun, Ra. If one carries over this transformation from green to gold to our tale, then it becomes evident that an essential aspect of the Great Mother has been constellated here that does indeed seek to assume a central position in conscious life.

Such a transformation seems to be accomplished in the course of the story through the birth of the children. The description of these children makes it clear that they represent an attempt to draw the realm of the green maiden, and especially that of the stag, the *golden* stag, into life. The first child has three *golden* curls. We know that the realm of gold belongs to the green maiden and is an expression of her importance.

Curls grow on their own, without the influence of our conscious thought and will. It is an autonomous process. Thus growing hair is often equated with the birth of ideas and the autonomous production of thoughts. This first child could be the expression of a first intimation that the realm of the green maiden also exists within oneself, the stag included, which is after all her active side, the side by which she can be drawn into life. Such an intimation could allow one to glimpse new potentialities in life.

On a quite practical level, this could simply refer to a woman's sudden intimation that she actually has the maternal element within her, that she need no longer seek it, that she is situated quite meaningfully in a relationship to life in which she has the capacity to give birth as well as to let go of her children, even when her external circumstances are not at all pleasant, that is, is not at all motherly.

However, this child is immediately taken away from the young woman. This knowledge full of intimations, which ushers in an enormous new beginning and signals the end of the frozen state, and which is thus meaningful and important like a new child—all this is what the green maiden takes back again. The new experience has taken place, but it cannot be maintained.

The green maiden steals the child, but here, in contrast to other comparable fairy tales, an entirely different attitude is present. For instance, in other tales, a black woman tears the child apart, or in a particularly brutal Italian version, the children are smashed against a wall. Here, however, the green maiden hugs and kisses the child. Just as earlier in the forest she seemed to need the broommaker's daughter, now she seems to need the child. But her child stealing is bound up with the question: "Did you see me in my distress?" By distress, she surely means the obstructed condition we have described. And the queen answers: "Dearest mother, I did not see you."

Let us look more closely at this act of discretion. Declaring the true nature of the divine green maiden would not have been to the point. If the maiden did not know who she really was, she never would have asked such a question. Thus the girl's response in no way indicates an oversight, but is instead connected with a certain attitude of the girl's toward the green maiden. The putative "not-having-seen" expresses the necessary respect, and addressing the green maiden as "dearest mother" relates to her through her good side. Although the young woman sees the green maiden stealing her child, there is obviously nothing she can say about it. In other tales, this is expressed in a more drastic fashion: the girl is struck mute, if not deaf and blind into the bargain. Here she offers the act of silence voluntarily.

This motif points to the importance of knowing the distress of the gods and not forgetting that they always have a side in need of salvation, and at the same time being discreet with this knowledge. This would be the fitting attitude that expresses the necessary respect. This attitude encompasses both the knowledge of their need to live through the actions and lives of humans and the consciousness of their vastly greater reach.

There is perhaps also another element here: If one experiences the ruthlessness of the gods as directly as here—if they intervene quite brutally in one's life—one needs to look away in order to continue being able to face life. In my opinion, in certain situations it is only the defense mechanism of not looking that can keep a person alive. But one has seen anyway.

This fairy tale focuses very strongly on the feeling that one is forced to be creative—to become a mother in the broadest sense—but that this cannot happen simply, because the archetypal mother has a fishtail and the little men accompanying her have stone legs.

Looking at this collectively, a woman must embrace the fate of her gender, but in the unique way that her inner nature demands, as a process of self-realization. And yet she must accept that the beginning of this process delivers nothing tangible. The green maiden takes the children away as soon as they are born.

Looked at from the other side, having the children taken away also indicates the necessity of letting things go. This, too, belongs to the sphere of motherhood. One receives the children and brings them into the world. One raises them, *has* them in a certain sense—and then they grow away. Being able to give them up is just as important as taking care of them.

In child-stealing figures in fairy tales one recognizes the myth of Lamia. After Lamia seduced Zeus, jealous Hera caused her to be able to bear only dead children.[5] Since then, she has menaced pregnant women, and stolen children and killed them. We also encounter the Great Mother as a goddess of death. At the same time, we see that behind this problem there is a "mother's curse."

The second child has a golden star on its chest. Here the gold is in a more central position than before. It is also clear under what star this child was born. Stars are distant lights, lights in the darkness, lights shining out of the unconscious. As inhabitants of the heavens, they have, as it were, a spiritual quality. If we did not already know by the symbol of gold alone that we have here a further incarnation of the golden stag, we could deduce it from this additional symbol, the sign under which this child is born.

The third child has the golden stag on its chest. We know from the beginning of the story that this golden stag always finds its way back to the green maiden; from the end of the story, we know that the golden stag is the bewitched king. Thus the child will find its way back and reappear.

With this child, the stag aspect becomes capable of entering life, though not completely, since this child is also taken back. This means that the stag-animus, whose most essential quality seems to be that he always guides and seduces us into further depths of the unconscious, is accepted. With that, the way to the Great Mother is open whenever he is called upon.

But now we come to the scene at the stake. Hitherto, we have had the feeling that though a boundless sadness has descended upon the queen, she nevertheless accepts what has happened. What else can she do? It is somewhat comparable to those psychological situations in which we keep sensing something of vital importance that we are completely unable to formulate or express. This is the sense of having to remain mute, that is, having important experiences but continuing to lose hold of them.

The people regard the queen as a cannibal, failing to perceive the process that is unfolding. The "people" is always an aspect of the personality—the part that looks on from the outside rather than really seeing what is happening. It is the collective aspect that has no feeling for the extraordinary since the extraordinary does not correspond to what is always and has always been done. Laborious attempts to tune in to an inner necessity take time and energy—the conscious world cannot be bothered. It is no wonder that one finally becomes furious and tries to put an end to this situation once and for all, thinking that since the whole situation is so fruitless, one is going to end it forever. That is what the "people" in oneself think. But fundamentally what is encountered here is a far more profound unconscious intention. The situation of wanting to have both the old and the new state of being cannot go on. Is the old persona going to remain or is a new ego going to develop? Is there really going to be a transformation? In the heroine's acceptance of the judgment of being burned at the stake, I see a readiness to let oneself be destroyed out of a sense of solidarity with this side of oneself, even when it has brought one nothing.

But it is just the persistence in this solidarity that brings liberation. This attitude toward her nature-bound self enables her to relate to the becoming and passing away that characterize the maternal situation—to love, fertility, nurturing, and death—and to learn to accept it all. It is in the moment of greatest conflict, the moment of the greatest menace, that the great transformation and the great rebirth begins: the children return to her. At the moment where she has proven at the possible cost of her life, in the face of death, that she takes this feminine-divine side of herself seriously, she receives the fruits of it. At that point, the green maiden is redeemed, she is also brought from an unripe state to a mature one. And the stag is redeemed as well.

The stag is the queen's husband. His redemption means that their relationship has now also been liberated, liberated from the hitherto unconscious femininity symbolized by the green maiden that the heroine carries within her and with which, up till now, she has approached the relationship. At the same time the masculine principle is liberated. Obviously the liberation of the feminine and the liberation of the masculine cannot be separated from each other.

Here the stag can be the heroine's *own* masculine side, but if we are interpreting the fairy tale as a collective process, it can also signify a general problem with the masculine principle. Fixation on the green maiden could mean psychological castration for the man, but the gold indicates that behind this fixation there is something of essential importance.

Let us attempt another overview. This fairy tale could very easily be seen as a puberty story, one that is bound up with the particular situation of the conscious world being somewhat frozen. But, if so, it is a puberty story in a very broad and collective sense, namely, the maturation process of an entire generation of women, or perhaps even several generations of women, who must take the direction given here, that of finding a new identity. The "cold" in this story is not only a time of year; the masculine element is still held in the domain of the Great Mother, and moreover in nonhuman form, that of the golden stag. Though a conscious awareness exists for a revitalized attitude toward nature, it is as an aspect of the unconscious that the green maiden becomes active: an archetype has been constellated that draws women under its spell. I am quite convinced that this is an appropriate image for today. It is most conspicuous perhaps in extremists of the women's movement who identify with the witch principle. Of course the question arises if it is really wise—and useful for the transformation of the witch archetype—to settle right into the witch's house. This fairy tale in particular concerns what is involved when one is in the house of an archetype. While recognizing the worth and dignity of it, one must realize that, without ever losing one's relationship to this archetype that has been constellated and has become the destiny of future generations, one must leave again. The problem indicated by the green maiden's fish tail is that for the time being the feminine principle *must* remain unconscious, since the creativity that is bound up with it is also frozen. The animus in this case has been transformed into a stag—a golden one, it is true, but all the same, a stag rather than a person—which as such is unable to function effectively in the real world; instead, with its seductive fascination, it draws us into an irrational realm. All of this is a consequence of the green maiden's exclusion from life.

We can also look at this story from a more individual perspective. A too-strong paternal bond can obstruct a girl's development into womanhood. To overcome this, it is essential for the golden stag, the seductive animus, to be drawn step by step into the real world—without any direct benefit for the girl at the outset. This means that the personal animus must undergo a development whereby it becomes distinct from the Great Mother. Everyone profits from this, especially the girl, who then becomes capable of relationship.

As long as this personal animus has not developed, everything will continue to be repossessed by the green maiden. The personal, not the collective, animus is absolutely necessary for the development of a personality that is capable of emancipating itself from the mother archetype to the extent necessary.

This individual interpretation is relatively easy to transpose into a collective one. We all know that nowadays many men have mother complexes. These "bewitched stags" definitely do exist in the real world today. Whether they are golden or not is another question. Let us assume that this fairy tale depicts a pattern of relationship in which both a man and a woman find themselves in the sphere of this constellating aspect of the Great Mother, and both of them project this whole world onto each other and want to have it fulfilled. In this perspective, the story speaks not primarily from the point of view of the man but from that of the woman. For her it is important in this situation to develop the animus in such a way as to become more independent and at the same time to grow away from the mother, so that the relationship with the man can at least be freed from the demand for motherliness. The personal animus also provides protection, so that the partnership between man and woman is not prevailed upon to provide more protection than each person can and must ordinarily provide for each other. A marriage should not be a protective institution but a real partnership.

The woman knows even at a distance that she is beholden to the archetype and even at the price of her life does not permit herself to be misled into losing her solidarity with it, because she sees in this solidarity her part in the developmental process of this archetype. Yet at the same time, through this process she clearly distinguishes herself from the archetype. And in this way, the man becomes freer as well.

It seems to me that the woman must take on the principal task here. In the encounter with the Great Mother, she is simply the one who is closest—it is her archetype, the archetype that is stands behind her identity.

I see this fairy tale as somewhat contrasting with "The Cursed Princess," which clearly shows where the man's growth and further development has to come into the picture.

It is remarkable that this fairy tale, whose narrative style unmistakably places it in the romantic period, so accurately expresses a present-day collective problem. Perhaps the reason for this is that ever and again similar constellations arise, which we of course interpret in terms of the archetypes that are constellated today— in me as well as you. In addition, it would be worthwhile to look

into what has become of the impulses that were set in motion in
the romantic period.

NOTES

1. August Ey (ed.), *Harzmärchen* (Stade, 1862). The first inspiration for
   the interpretation of this tale came from Marie-Louise von Franz's
   essay "Bei der schwarzen Frau" (In the House of the Black Woman),
   in Laiblin (ed.), *Märchenforschung und Tiefenpsychologie*, pp. 324ff.
2. "Die schwarze Frau," in *Märchen aus dem Donaulande* (Jena, 1926).
3. According to the *Handwörterbuch des deutschen Aberglaubens* (Dic-
   tionary of German Superstitions), green birch rods are regarded as
   wands of life, having a pronounced life-giving function.
4. Karl Kerényi, *The Gods of the Greeks* (Baltimore: Penguin Books,
   1958), p. 75.
5. Cf. C. G. Jung, *Symbole der Wandlung* (Symbols of Transformation,
   CW 5), p. 318.

INGRID RIEDEL

The Smith's Daughter
Who Knew How to Hold
Her Tongue

On the Problem of Suffering

What appears on the individual level as the complex of a
girl psychologically damaged by a suicidal father—a complex that can be cleared up only through an encounter with
the Great Mother—appears on the collective level as a complex of our entire Christian-influenced culture. The dark,
nature-bound side of the feminine principle has become
split off, and along with it the emotional side of men, which
includes artistic and religious experience. This fairy tale
shows a significant transformation in the realm of the Great
Feminine, which also promises to liberate buried masculine
values. The importance of this transformation can be seen
in the fact that many parallels exist in fairy tales from all
over the European cultural sphere. In this tale, as in many of
the others, the protagonist who sets the transformation process in motion is a girl, which makes sense in that this transformation proceeds from the archetype of the feminine.

The following fairy tale has plot patterns similar to the
previous ones. But since the initial situation is very different,
that is, since the psychic problem is very differently constellated, behind similar actions in the plot we find different
developmental processes. Just as we should not see behind a
symbol only an interpretation but rather let the symbol remain independent of what it has evoked, in the same way we
should not regard fairy tales as confined to a single interpre-

tation. The fairy tale remains independent of both teller and interpreter.

Once upon a time, there was a poor smith whose entire fortune consisted of an old ramshackle hut, a wife, and a host of hungry children. With his last seven pennies he bought himself a rope, for he wanted to hang himself. He went into the forest, picked out a strong branch, and knotted the rope to it.

No sooner was it tied on than a black woman appeared before him as though she had sprung out of the ground and said to him: "Smith, don't do that!"

The smith got frightened and untied the rope, and the black woman vanished. As soon as she was gone, he started to tie the rope back onto the branch.

But immediately the black woman appeared again, shook her finger at him threateningly, and said: "Didn't I tell you, smith, that you should leave off?"

The smith untied the rope once more and started home. But on the way he said to himself: "At home there's nothing left to eat. I prefer to hang myself."

He again looked for a strong branch and once again began to tie his rope to it.

But once more the black woman popped up in front of him as though she had sprung out of the ground. "Why won't you listen to me, smith?" she demanded.

"What good is it to listen to you? We're all going to have to die of hunger anyhow."

"You won't die of hunger," replied the black woman, "because I'm going to give you as much money as you want—on condition that you give me something that is in your house that you don't know about anyway."

The smith was astonished at these strange words, but when the black woman handed him a huge sack full of gold pieces, he thanked her profoundly and went home as fast as his legs would carry him.

"But don't forget your promise about what you have at home that you don't know about that belongs to me," the black woman repeated. "In seven years I'll be back to get it."

"I know very well what's in my house," said the smith, smiling. "And if by any chance there's something there that I don't know about yet, you're welcome to it." When the smith got home, he carefully piled up the gold pieces, which made a giant heap. Then his happiness was immense as well.

"Our little Goldilocks has brought us luck," said the smith's wife, and she showed her husband a very beautiful baby girl who had golden hair and a golden star on her forehead. She was the smith's youngest daughter, who had just been born.

Suddenly the smith became very sad, for now he understood what the black woman had been talking about.

The years went by, and Goldilocks became a very pretty little girl, to both the happiness and chagrin of her parents. When she was seven years old, a black carriage stopped in front of the house and the black woman climbed out of it.

"I've come to fetch your little girl," she said to the smith. She took the little girl by the hand and put her into the carriage. The parents, the brothers, the sisters all cried and pleaded in vain. The black woman wouldn't change her mind. The black driver cracked his whip, and at once the black carriage began to roll.

On and on they rolled, passing through lonely, forsaken regions and dark forests, and finally stopped in front of a black castle.

"This black castle belongs to you," said the black woman to Goldilocks. "There are a hundred rooms in this castle. You can have a look at all of them except the last. If you go into that one, it will go ill with you. I'll visit you again in seven years." And the black woman rode away in the black carriage.

Goldilocks was not unhappy. She was mistress of ninety-nine rooms. She didn't look into the hundredth room once.

And before she knew it, the seven years were up.

One day the black woman appeared in her coach and asked the girl: "Have you been in the last room?"

"No," our Goldilocks answered without lying.

"You did well to listen to me. In seven years I'll be back again. If you obey me again this time, I will make you a very happy girl. But if you go into the hundredth room, be ready for a fate worse than death." After the black woman had uttered this threat, she got back into her black coach and disappeared for seven years.

These seven years passed swiftly. The day on which the black woman was to come arrived. And Goldilocks was very happy, for the black woman would certainly congratulate and reward her. But suddenly she heard marvelous music. "Who is playing so beautifully in this castle?" Goldilocks asked herself. She started off in the direction from which the music was coming and arrived in front of the hundredth room. She opened the door without being aware of it at all and stood on the threshold, dazed: Twelve black men were sitting around a table, and a thirteenth was standing.

"Goldilocks, little Goldilocks, what have you done!" the thirteenth cried.

Her fear was so great that her heart nearly stopped beating. "What must I do now?" she murmured.

"Tell no one even a word of what you have seen here whatever might happen. This is the only way you can attain forgiveness for your mistake."

Goldilocks closed the door to the room—and in that very moment she heard the black coach roll up in front of the castle.

"What did you see in the hundredth room?" asked the black woman, who knew right away what had happened.

Goldilocks silently shook her head.

"Good, then. If you won't speak, you will be mute from

now on. You will only be able to talk to me," scolded the black woman, and she chased the girl from the castle.

Goldilocks walked until she fell down from sheer fatigue. She had come to a beautiful, very green meadow. She stretched out on the grass, wept a great deal, and then fell asleep.

Then the young king of the country, who had been hunting nearby, rode past the meadow and saw the young girl sleeping. She was so beautiful that he was immediately seized by a great love for her. Despite her muteness, he took her up on his horse and brought her to his castle. Not long after, he married her, and she became queen.

Goldilocks lived happily in the castle, and a year later she brought a son into the world who had golden hair and a golden star on his forehead. The entire castle joyously celebrated the birth of the prince.

But the first night, the black woman paid a visit to the young queen and threatened her in the following words: "If you don't tell me right away what you saw in the hundredth room, I'll kill your son."

Goldilocks was at the height of despair, but nevertheless she remembered what the thirteenth man had promised her: if she remained silent, she would be forgiven. Goldilocks shook her head and remained silent.

The black woman seized the newborn child from the cradle, killed it, and smeared its blood on Goldilocks's mouth.

Then she disappeared with the dead child.

The following morning everyone was horrified to see the blood on the queen's mouth.

"Is it possible that she ate her child?" everybody asked himself, full of horror. But no one dared to bring forth such an accusation. Not even the king himself. And Goldilocks was still mute.

A year later, Goldilocks brought a little girl into the world. She had golden hair and a star on her forehead. The castle folk were very happy, but all were afraid that the little girl might disappear like her little brother the year before. Therefore the king posted a guard in front of Goldilocks's chamber—but it was in vain. During the night, the black woman came again.

"If you don't tell me what you saw in the hundredth room of the castle, I'll kill your child," she said in a menacing voice.

Goldilocks cried hard, shook her head, and said nothing.

The black woman took the little girl, killed her, and smeared Goldilocks's mouth with the blood of her child. Then she vanished with the little corpse.

On the following morning, everyone in the castle was seized with horror when they learned the news, and the king ordered that the queen be burned in front of the castle.

Goldilocks cried hard, but because she was mute, she could not defend herself, and no one had pity on her.

As Goldilocks appeared next to the heap of wood that the executioners had prepared on the edge of the town, the black woman came again. "Will you tell me now what you saw in the hundredth room?" she asked. "If you don't tell me, you will be burned alive."

But this time, too, Goldilocks shook her head and held her tongue.

So the executioners bound Goldilocks to the stake and lit the fire. But as the flames approached her feet, the black woman suddenly turned completely white and screamed imploringly: "Put out the fire, put out the fire!"

Everyone got frightened, and the executioners put out the fire. The white woman had a little boy and a little girl come out of the coach. Both had golden hair and a star on the forehead. She pushed them toward Goldilocks and said to her: "By holding your tongue, you have brought me and yourself happiness and fortune. You have saved us all." At once she vanished.

The king hardly believed his eyes and ears as he saw all

that and as Goldilocks recounted what had befallen her. Beside himself with joy, he took Goldilocks back to the castle and had the smith, his wife, and all his children brought as well.

And they all lived happily until they died.[1]

THE PRELIMINARY STORY:
FROM THE PERSPECTIVE OF THE SMITH

In the figure of the smith we find reflected a masculine component of the psyche, which in dealing with life depends primarily on physical outer strength and skill, hard labor (but in connection with the "transformational elements" fire and metal), and naive, unbroken vitality (the big family). In the case of this "poor" smith, we should probably think of a basic type of smith who, for example, shoes horses, rather than of a fine smith, such as Hephaestos or Wieland the Smith. However, like them, he is "crippled." And that is quite significant, since after all the trade of smith is one of the creative trades and is thus related to the creative forces.

The relatively primitive approach of consciousness characteristic of the smith is presented here as dilapidated. All that remains of his "fortune" consists of an "old ramshackle hut." Psychologically, this means that the container of this approach toward life is now worn out. Somehow, too, it is the smith who has let it degenerate.

The smith has a wife, who does not leave him, but remains bound to him, not least because of the "host of hungry children." So there are children there, youthful forces, which the smith in his current situation and state of mind can no longer feed. He believes, in his resignation and depression, that they are all doomed to die of hunger.

Nevertheless, it is to be noted that the poverty of the smith must not have arisen through his own fault—the fairy tale tells us nothing of the sort—but rather as a result of general conditions. What he is no longer able to provide is food for himself and his family. Thus he is remiss in his masculine, fatherly protection of his family, the care that is also a maternal duty. This is the situation that drives the smith into extreme resignation and depression. He uses his last seven coins (equivalent to the last few ounces of his strength) to buy a rope, with which he has decided to hang himself. Though it is not necessary to discuss in depth the symbolism of the number seven, we could perhaps go as far as to relate it to the seven-year phases that mark the development of the girl. Thus the seven coins could simply be an expression of the last phase of the smith's worn-out attitude or approach to life. This phase is determined by the figure of the smith alone, whereas the next phases are determined in common by the maturing girl and the dark woman.

The smith's decision to put an end to his old life drives him into the forest to look for a branch capable of bearing the burden of his life to which he can tie the rope, the thread of his destiny. Inwardly, he is "down," "grounded," at the lowest point of his existence. Then a strange synchronicity occurs: As he is tying the rope to the branch, a black woman appears before him "as though she had sprung from the ground." A new compensating psychic energy rises out of the ground of his stagnation, an opposed energy, feminine as opposed to his old, one-sidedly masculine smith's approach to life, which is oriented toward everyday situations. And it is just this energy that puts an end to his decision to destroy himself. The intimation of wondrous, extraordinary possibilities of action and deliverance that are connected with the appearance of this figure, and that become psychologically real, cause him to stop. He does not find them convincing, it is true, until the third time, after the black woman asks him severely, "Why won't you listen to me, smith?" (Here the narrator also calls the listener's attention to the fact that up until now the smith has been unwilling to heed the voice of the dark feminine principle, that it has remained alien to him. He also did not allow her to appeal to his conscience or change his mind.) He replies: "What good is it to listen to you? We're all going to have to die of hunger anyhow."

Only when the woman promises a remedy for the hunger, and when she gives him something on the spot—gold!—and in this way shows her motherliness, does he take her seriously, and his depression yields to "immense happiness." This is an interesting switch. Doesn't this drastic changeability from deep depression to impetuous happiness indicate a rather childish character structure?

The black woman's color characterizes her as earthy, chthonic. As a chthonic figure, she has the riches of the earth—gold—available to her. Apart from her appearance in this tale, the precise form of the black woman appears only in a variation from the Danube valley, "In the House of the Black Woman."[2] In many variants—for example, in "The Green Maiden"—this character is green, which places her more in the realm of vegetation.[3]

Black and gold are the two contrasting colors that move through the entire tale. Whole semantic fields develop around these two colors. Gold is in the "sack full of gold pieces," in the name Goldilocks, and in the golden hair and gold stars on the foreheads of the children. At the same time we repeatedly find the idea of luck connected with the color gold.

The color black in turn appears within its semantic field in the black woman, the black carriage, the black driver, the black coach, the black castle, and the twelve black men. Also to be included are the dark forests through which the coach drives and the dark night during which the black woman appears to the new mother. The two semantic fields "gold" and "black" are mysteriously bound up with each other. It is the black woman, after all, who, in the first scene, gives the smith the life-saving gold. Being black—the color symbolic of inhibition and melancholy—she embodies the depression that is often experienced in the psycho-therapeutic process as a "gold-producing" introverted state. From the semantic field "black" to the semantic field "gold" runs the need for deliverance and the process of deliverance of the black woman herself. Her blackness means not only that she belongs to the earth realm, but also that she is cursed, shadowed, evil. The corresponding figure in a parallel Italian variant[4] is called "the evil woman." In "Do You Confess?" she is called "the witch." In our tale, as well as in the corresponding variant "In the House of the Black Woman," the black woman must be redeemed. She must become white through a quasi-alchemical transformation from the nigredo to the albedo. The catalyst of the transformation is the girl.

With all her ambivalence, the smith encounters the black woman as a provider and savior. The psychic energy embodied in the black woman is able, shortly after her first appearance, to preserve the smith from a deadly depression. At the same time it becomes clear that in the future the "black-woman factor" must be reckoned as part of his life. She calls him to account for the life-saving "advance" of gold, happiness, and new opportunities in life that she provided him with at the time of her first appearance. His acquisition of the rope ended up tying him to her.

In the second scene as well, from the smith's return home to the point when the black woman takes his daughter away, the smith is portrayed as quite unconscious. This is indicated by the fact that she has to remind him of his promise immediately after his return home. At the same time the formulation of her condition, "what you have at home that you don't know about that belongs to me," expresses that the smith does not clearly know what he has, what is within him. And part of this picture of un-consciousness is his naive certainty that he has clear knowledge about the interior of his house: "'I know very well what's in my house,' said the smith smiling. 'And if by any chance there's something there that I don't know about yet, you're welcome to it.'" His smile also shows that he has not realized what a fateful entanglement with the black woman he has gotten himself into. Just as, at the beginning, he naively fell prey to his depression, he now surrenders himself to his happiness over the mountain of gold, the psychic "cost" of which he hides from himself, repressing it for the time being.

The narrator then skillfully connects the smith's naive happiness about the gold with a shocking turn of events. The listener still knows nothing, no more than the smith, about what mysterious thing might be found in the house. Unexpectedly, "our little Goldilocks" is mentioned, and indeed, mentioned as the first thing within a new interpretive field, that of the smith's wife, the mother: "Our little Goldilocks has brought us luck." This is the way we learn that a youngest daughter has just been born to the smith, a daughter with "golden hair and a golden star on her forehead." Through this presentation, the listener participates in the surprise and horror of the smith. A synchronistic event has taken place: the smith's death wish, the appearance of the black woman, and the birth of "little Goldilocks" all coincide temporally (at least in fairy tale time, which is also that of psychological events). In this perspective the smith's wife was right: the birth of Goldilocks was the unknown new potentiality of the smith's, which is what brought him luck.

Psychologically, this could mean that the smith, in seeking to put an end to his old approach to life with its lack of wonder, rescues the black woman from her absorption in the unconscious. Her appearance, itself the birth of a new possibility, prepares the way for the birth of Goldilocks.

Psychic energy never appears out of nowhere like a deus ex machina; it always works within an area of tension in the psychic energy system. Here this tension is between the light-colored young feminine potential—Goldilocks—and the unredeemed dark feminine principle constellated by the dark action of the smith. This light feminine potential will become free only when it has liberated the dark feminine (along with the dark masculine) principle. The smith component of the psyche has been only provisionally saved from self-destruction; it is not yet liberated. First it must "sacrifice" its new creative potential (Goldilocks) to serve the dark woman, which means another depressive phase, since the potential has not yet been understood and integrated. "The parents, the brothers, the sisters all cried and pleaded in vain. The black woman wouldn't change her mind."

In contrast to the girl in "Do You Confess?," whose precocious supernatural powers and initiatory visit to the witch at the age of fifteen show her to be a true witch's daughter, Goldilocks is portrayed as a human child who relates passively to being carried off at a tender age. Her special features are her golden locks and the golden star on her forehead. This child, who was born "simultaneously" with her father's decision to kill himself and his meeting with the black woman, is particularly associated with light or brilliance. Blond, in mythology, is the hair color of gods of light such as Baldur and heroes such as Siegfried. In Western painting, the Christ Child is depicted with golden curls, with the fateful Christmas star shining above him. This is the golden star on the forehead. It is placed over the seat of consciousness, on the spot where Hinduism and Buddhism localize higher consciousness. This is where Brahmins wear their sign of nobility, this is where the spiritual "third eye" is located. Thus this child, the daughter of a crude, unconscious smith, is marked for higher consciousness by her star of destiny. As we shall see in the course of the fairy tale, this child is so strongly marked by the light principle that she will need a longer time ($3 \times 7 = 21$ years) and stronger temptation (she is drawn by wondrous music) than other comparable fairy tale heroines to bring her to cross the threshold into darkness. But she needs this initiation into darkness in order to be able to redeem the dark woman as well as her dark father.

THE MAIN PART:
FROM THE PERSPECTIVE OF GOLDILOCKS

Following the rather long sequence that is experienced from the point of view of the father, the smith, the perspective of the narrative shifts to the point of view of Goldilocks, the daughter. If we were to stick with the initial vantage point from within masculine psychology, this shift would be to the anima.

However, it is also open to us to change our perspective, as the narrator of the tale does, and experience the rest of the development of the tale from the perspective of the feminine component, "Goldilocks." In doing this we would understand the initial scenes concerning the father as an exposition of the psychic constellation under which the actions and experiences of the feminine ego take place. A young girl who grows up under such a constellation lacks the experience of finding shelter and protection in her father. She is more likely to feel that she is "father's great hope," a substitute that makes up for what the father himself cannot accomplish. The masculine principle must seem rather mercurial and undependable to such a girl. A negative father complex is a strong possibility.

The narrator's choice of perspective leaves us no choice but to empathize with this girl who is carried off at the age of seven by the black woman in her black coach. In our tale there is no mention of horses, as there is in "Do You Confess?," nor is there any indication that the coach is pulled by ghosts rather than horses as in the tale "In the House of the Black Woman." This coach is set in motion by a black driver cracking his whip. Like Charon, the mythical ferryman, this coach driver guides the wagon through the border region into the dark underworld. Thus he shares a fateful element with "the coachman in front" (behind whom the coachman Chronos hides) in the "Song of the Yellow Wagon": "I would be so happy to stay, but the wagon she is rolling." Thus the girl's destiny has begun to roll irreversibly, as the double repetition of the word *roll* in two succeeding sentences emphasizes. And when it says, "On and on they rolled, passing through lonely, forsaken regions and dark forests, and finally stopped in front of a black castle," this portrays the transition from the region of consciousness we have been in until now to another completely unknown one. The categories that are used here—the temporal ones, such as "on and on," and the spatial ones, such as "passing through lonely, forsaken regions and dark forests"—are only auxiliary concepts that help guide our imagination into another dimension remote from consciousness.

The notion of "forsaken" regions, like the motif of the castle overgrown with forest, hints at a former phase of culture, an earlier stage of collective consciousness, which has now sunk below the threshold of consciousness. But the expression "forsaken regions" could also mean that these places never have been cultivated.

In terms of the personal psychology of the little girl, this must mean that she is being brought into remote archetypal realms of the collective feminine, with which in her seven years of consciousness development she could never have come in contact (unless it was via the mother imago). Her personal mother, the smith's wife, who has an inkling of the exceptional destiny of "our little Goldilocks"—she was the first to refer to it—tries, crying and pleading, to block this. However, she seems to have no basic contact with the realm of the dark feminine. After all, the smith falls into despair despite her presence, and can only be saved by what seems to be a completely alien manifestation of the dark aspect. His wife seems to be all too passive and colorless.

For Goldilocks, then, the encounter with the black woman and the abduction to her castle signifies her first encounter with the powerful dark mother imago.

Symbolically, the castle is analogous to the black woman herself. It not only shares her coloring but also her curse. It stands out from other similar tales in that the black woman immediately and definitively gives the castle to the girl: "This castle belongs to you." What elsewhere is only partially initiated by handing over the keys, and then only "on trial," what elsewhere is only to be awarded after the most difficult tests have been passed, is here granted at once. In the first instance, the black woman appears to the girl, as to the father, as the generous gift giver, the Great Mother in her giving aspect. Only her black color hints at the entanglements to come. The gift of the whole castle to the seven-year-old girl expresses the inheritance of her entire feminine self in potential form; it now belongs to her, though its actualization is something she still must earn. This feminine self is still unexplored and shrouded in darkness, as though under a spell. This corresponds to the black woman's suggestion to the girl to have a look at all hundred of the rooms, one after the other, except the last one. The girl can and should learn about all her inner realms, which would be to her benefit, with the exception of the last one: "If you go into that one, it will go ill with you." A threat of misfortune and suffering hangs over this last room. Seven years are given to the girl for the initial exploration of the castle. This is the crucial period for the development of her womanhood, between the ages of seven and fourteen. For the duration of this period, the black woman, including her black coach, will leave her alone. This is a way of saying that the dark aspect of the feminine will spare her during this phase, allowing her a peaceful period of development. After the first seven-year phase of childhood spent with her parents, brothers, and sisters, made carefree by the black woman's gift of gold, comes a second seven-year phase to be spent under the spell of the archetypal feminine. During this period she is relatively alone—this is characteristic of this phase in developmental psychology—but "not unhappy." In her way, she is rich: she is "mistress of ninety-nine rooms." This is the phase of far-flung fantasy during which nearly every girl builds "castles in the air" in which she makes room for her own inner world; but as long as she does not violate the taboos set by the mother imago—and she does not yet need to break them—it is not necessary for her to become involved with the dark side of her feminine nature.

On the other hand, the unredeemed progressive energy embodied in the dark woman lies in wait for the girl and encourages her to break the taboo. After another seven years, in the girl's fourteenth year (the age at which most fairy tale heroines break the taboo), the black woman enticingly inquires if the girl has been in the hundredth room. Or is this an unfair suspicion? Could the black woman herself be so unconscious that she does not see the ambivalence of her ostensibly motherly scrutiny? Should the psychic potency embodied in the black woman be conceived of as her unawareness of her need for deliverance, or is she carefully hiding it, as in the variant "In the House of the Black Woman"?

This question cannot be answered on the basis of the text, but it directs our attention to the strategic technique of the narrator, who never wastes a word on the inner intentions of the black woman: that would not fit the narrative style of fairy tales, which never give us any insight into the inner workings of their characters but merely depict their interrelationships in a strictly functional way. Through lines like "'No,' our Goldilocks answered without lying," the narrator calls our attention to the possibility of violating the ban and then having to lie about it. The listener's attention is drawn to the existence of this temptation primarily by the black woman's return at seven-year intervals. The listener, too, is gripped by curiosity and an urge to violate the ban. At points like this, it is particularly transparent that the narrator is using a psychological technique that makes the listener a participant, an accomplice to the crime, and a possible recipient of psychic liberation in the end as well.

Now the black woman's ban is formulated again, this time in a particularly convincing manner. The girl is promised happiness itself if she can maintain the taboo for another seven years. It is emphasized that "you have done well to listen to me." This might well remind the listener of the father at the beginning being asked in a reprimanding tone, "Why won't you listen to me?" For the smith, listening to the black woman turned out to have a life-saving result. Thus it seems like a logical inversion for the black woman to threaten: "But if you go into the hundredth room, be ready for a fate worse than death."

Goldilocks is already basking in being a "good girl," still childlike and innocent at twenty-one years of age—doesn't this point to a retardation in development?—by the time the day arrives, at the end of the third seven-year phase, when the black woman is to return: "And Goldilocks was very happy, for the black woman would certainly congratulate and reward her."

In the midst of feeling good about the goal nearly achieved, she encounters something unexpected in this castle, which must be imagined as a quiet and deserted place. She hears some marvelous music. Here, as in dreams, music is connected with feelings on the verge of bursting forth. The feeling function, which we haven't seen up till now, announces itself. This function, when it is unfamiliar and unexercised, can bring confusion to the prevailing orientation. Thus in an Irish fairy tale, wonderful music comes rising out of a fairy mound and lures the hero into it, where he forgets time and space and is lost. The Lorelei's song draws sailors to ruin.

Here also the girl loses the orientation she has had until now through the magic of this music that she obviously has not heard before ("Who is playing so beautifully in this castle?") and through the emotion arising in her, and she immediately pursues this mysterious new reference point. And unlike all other fairy tale heroines pursuing the object of their curiosity, she opens the door of the last room involuntarily—"without being aware of it at all"—and remains standing on the threshold, more astonished than horrified (the text says "dazed," which is quite different from the speechless horror in "Graycoat" or the even worse horror in "Do You Confess?"). Here also there are no corpses. Instead, "twelve black men were sitting around a table, and a thirteenth was standing." This image takes us by complete surprise since she had imagined herself to be all alone as mistress of the castle, just as her father had imagined himself in his hut. Here we have a repetition of the psychological motif that there are other inhabitants in one's inner house of whom consciousness knows nothing. The image is mysterious and at first glance impenetrable. It is noteworthy that again all are clothed in black. This girl, who has been here in this castle since her seventh year as a result of the pact made by her father with the black woman, has never, as the narrator tacitly suggests, beheld anything male since that time. The world of the masculine has become completely split off from her. The initial reaction of these men who are suddenly no longer taboo is astonishing. The thirteenth, the one who is standing, calls Goldilocks by name, as if calling to a sleepwalker: "Goldilocks, little Goldilocks, what have you done!" This sounds more sympathetically frightened than angry. By knowing her name, he hints at and establishes subliminal contact between Goldilocks and all of these men. And only now does she become aware of her deed, and of the relationship between this and the black woman's prohibition. Only now does her fear become comparable to that of other fairy tale heroines when they have opened the forbidden chamber: "Her fear was so great that her heart nearly stopped beating." Thus she was nearly frightened to death.

So the main thing that touches her so directly, along with the taboo violation, is being addressed and already known by the dark figures. The most noteworthy element here, something that is not repeated in any of the other variants, is that in the midst of her fear, she turns to the very figure of whom she had been so frightened and asks, "What must I do now?" Here we finally have a manifestation of the character of this girl; hitherto we have known very little outside of her association with the light principle and her childish purity and lack of experience. Now we see that she trusts the dark aspect once she finds out that she is known and recognized by it. So she unburdens herself to the black men she has discovered, and begs them, rather than the black woman, for advice. The further course of the tale shows us that she has unconditional trust in these thirteen dark men, the spokesman as well as the other twelve. The thirteenth advises her: "Tell no one even a word of what you have seen here, whatever might happen. This is the only way you can attain forgiveness for your mistake."

We are soon shown that there is more involved in the girl's long-destined embroilment with the dark aspect than a mistake that has to be forgiven; we see that it is an indispensable step in a development that brings about transformation in all the participating elements. The girl does not know this. She is only aware of a trespass in relation to the black woman. She places her trust in the advice of the thirteenth dark man, who knows her by name, and in relating to the black woman keeps her discovery a secret. This group of men displays the precise characteristics of a split-off complex. Being called by name might have the effect of a secret sign of recognition: "I have called thee by name; thou art mine," says Yahweh to his prophet. The girl's trust, which is still hard to understand, also seems to be related to the music emanating from the men's room. She seems to be bound to them by a musical secret, an emotional secret for which words neither exist nor are necessary. Now for the first time the girl is no longer following the external command of the black woman but is following her own feeling, which distinguishes her from the black woman; but at the same time she must serve the black woman's deepest intentions, the latter's own liberation from the spell of the dark aspect: "The heart has its reasons, which reason knows not" (Pascal). What seems essential in this action is that here the girl takes a decisive step out of her servitude to the black woman.

That this step at the same time moves her into a secret solidarity with the cursed men is the other side of the same constellation.

Again we have a remarkable synchronicity. The girl who belongs so strongly to the principle of light can only break the taboo on the last day, when the black woman's coach is already rolling up. Forces belonging to the psychic potency represented by the black woman permit this step into apparently disorienting emotion. When these forces become integrated, the daughter-anima will be able to disentangle herself from the mother and establish her independence.

THE FORBIDDEN ROOM

The actual content of the hundredth room requires separate consideration. We have twelve black men sitting around a table and a thirteenth who is standing. A closely associated analogy from the world of European fairy tales that strongly suggests itself is the twelve fairies in "Brier Rose" ("Sleeping Beauty," Grimm's no. 50) who were joined by a thirteenth, the uninvited one. This thirteenth fairy, because of her initial exclusion—the fairy tale says this explicitly—became Sleeping Beauty's evil fairy. But it is precisely in this capacity that she sets the whole action of the fairy tale in motion.

Another analogy is that of the thirteenth chamber, which appears in many fairy tales instead of the hundredth as the tabooed room. Here in our fairy tale, the meaning of the thirteenth as the tabooed room has obviously been transferred to the contents of the room. The number thirteen has remained under such a taboo in the general consciousness that modern hotels sometimes do not dare use it as a room number; instead they offer their guests the same room under the number 12A.

Among European variants known to me, the thirteen men are unique as inhabitants of the tabooed room; this uniqueness suggests that a later collective content has been added to a basic tale (such as "Graycoat" or "Do You Confess?"). In such cases, it is often illuminating to consider contents from the Christian tradition, since these have had a strong retroactive effect on the collective unconscious of the European peoples. And indeed, a central motif from the Christian tradition presents itself here, one that seems to be reflected even on the level of detail. This is the motif of the Last Supper, where Jesus sits at table with his twelve disciples. Indeed, the fairy tale highlights just that moment in the scene at which Judas, the future traitor, is told to leave: "What you are going to do, do quickly."

Judas would then be the thirteenth, the one standing up, the supernumerary, the disinvited disciple—in short, the evil one—analogous to the evil fairy in the Sleeping Beauty tale.

This amplification could still be considered far-fetched if a more precise parallel were not at hand: Judas is the disciple who hanged himself after the betrayal, just as the smith intended to hang himself at the beginning of our fairy tale. That this attempted deed of her father's could well appear to the girl again in the tabooed room is shown by the fairy tale "Do You Confess?," which contains a related motif. In that tale, the girl actually finds a corpse in the tabooed room with a copper wire around its neck, copper suggesting the coins the smith used to buy the rope in the first place. Here it is clear that the content of the tabooed room is confronting the girl with the initial event of the story—her father's attempts at suicide.

A further striking analogy between this corpse and the thirteenth man in our tale is that this corpse, like the thirteenth man, gives the girl the saving advice to divulge nothing of what has happened. "Tell no one even a word of what you have seen here." Here, too, the girl trusts and holds fast to this advice to the bitter end.

At the end of both these tales, we are given the news, which is not all that common in fairy tales, that the girl renews her contact with her father, as if to say that now all has come full circle and the relationship to the father has been resolved.

Thus, were we to see in the thirteenth man an encounter with the dark, suicidal aspect of her father, we would still only have one piece of a very complicated puzzle. The father decides to put an end to the unbearable situation at the beginning of the fairy tale by betraying his family and hanging himself. In this way he triggers the denouement of the redemptive drama of the fairy tale, just as Judas, also through betrayal and hanging, set the Christian redemptive drama in motion.

We should further note that the thirteenth is also found as an ambivalent figure elsewhere than in this fairy tale. In the Judaic tradition of the Kabbalah, thirteen is the embodiment of the spirit of evil.[6] The thirteenth chapter of the Book of Revelation in the Christian tradition contains the description of the Antichrist and the evil one. Judas is here characterized as unequivocally evil. Later on, a new twelfth disciple was chosen in his place; in this way he definitively became the supernumerary, the excluded one. His death at his own hand was proscribed by the Christian church; suicides were denied a Christian burial for centuries.

According to the arhythmo-symbology of Allendy,[7] thirteen is an active principle, which would accord quite well with the fact that the thirteenth man is standing while the twelve others are sitting. He is caught in the act of departure, perhaps en route to betrayal. But in this way he sets the decisive phase of the Christian redemptive drama in motion. Certain modern Christian exegetes believe that Judas did not want to annihilate Jesus, but rather to challenge him and finally force him into action and make him reveal himself in his full power. To Judas the process of the redemptive drama appeared to have stagnated. What Allendy says about the significance of thirteen as an active number accords with this view: one who comes in the thirteenth place is a creature who fails to act in harmony with the universal laws for which the twelve stand. Was not Judas's deed, like all comparable acts performed by evil fairies, or witches, or Mephisto, the act of a self-willed creature, serving, from the perspective of individual psychology, that universal law characterized by Mephisto in *Faust* as "a part of that force that always seeks evil and always engenders good"?

Our tale seems to reflect this theme in its own fashion. Judas's deed, which in the last analysis also includes his hanging himself, has been tabooed by the collective consciousness. For that reason, the entire scene here is bathed in black. The communality of the twelve men at table, their communion, their relationship with the sacred—all has fallen under taboo. It is obvious that it is from this deep and tender dimension of spiritual-emotional communality that the wonderful music emanated that attracted the girl to intrude into the forbidden room. The feminine element seems initially to be entirely lacking from this communality, just as it was long excluded from the priesthood of the Christian church and lacked altogether a "metaphysical representation" (in Jung's words) in Christianity. On the other hand, the feminine is present here in the reality of the *communio* ("communion," or creating community by, for instance, sharing a common meal, is part of the feminine symbolic domain). In the same way, the feminine element later established itself in Christianity in the form of the community of the "Mother Church," which was further embodied in the Virgin Mary. It was not least because this entire dimension was lacking for him that the smith was led to hang himself: *communio* would never have permitted such a desperate act of isolation to arise.

Nevertheless, the immediate impression conveyed by this scene definitely remains valid: we have an exclusively male group before us; the concrete manifestation of the feminine, the woman, appears as an intruder. Although the reaction to her is a knowing one, at the same time it is one of shock.

Only when we have taken in this state of affairs do we fully appreciate the secret complicity that now arises between the group of men—or the thirteenth man, to be more precise—and the girl. Understanding the situation from the point of view of masculine psychology (that of the smith), we see that there is a central complex, emotionally emphasized (by the music) but split off—the complex of the betrayed sacred community of men, the *communio* in the spiritual domain—that is suddenly exposed by the intrusion of the anima. The hidden wholeness of the psyche (the number twelve), which is betrayed and sold out by the thirteenth, who hangs himself, is rediscovered. And the traitor himself, who must know what he is talking about because he himself is overcome by despair following his violation of the taboo, now advises the anima: "Tell no one even a word of what you have seen here." These men are not masters of their own house, but in their split-off situation are dependent on the work of the feminine anima: clearly it is she who, through her steadfast silence, must redeem the betrayal that has brought these men into the domain of the taboo.

Now let us look at this situation from the point of view of feminine psychology. The girl Goldilocks learns that this dark masculine mystery is hidden in her castle, that is, in her own inner sphere. She is not the mistress of her own feminine realm, because an unresolved collective masculine problem is haunting her hundredth room. It is the masculine aspect that is initially more or less split off in every feminine psyche that must be integrated through increasing maturity. Making contact with this aspect is indispensable for the development of a relationship to a real man, especially for this daughter with a negative father complex (which of course the group of black men also represents). And it is also a condition for the development of a connection with the spiritual, with the animus in its many aspects.

The taboo here obviously goes further and has deeper roots than what is involved in a female ego's effort to develop into the sexual role indicated by our culture and therefore initially repressing its masculine potentialities. The content of this room in its *collective* aspect points beyond this to the fact that there is something unresolved and unredeemed in the masculine realm itself. Let us again take the point of view that the twelve men at the table represent a male *communio* configured around a central religious figure, Christ. A priestly male community analogous to this was the main bearer of European culture for hundreds of years. But Judas had already potentially disrupted it at the Last Supper by creating a breach, an entry point for darkness into this light-oriented communality. Now he crops up once again in the fairy tale, perhaps to point out that now in the hallowed, closed male community of light a breach has once again been made, that the time has come to look at what has hitherto been excluded and condemned, to redeem Judas and include him in an expanded, more complex Christian consciousness.

As the spokesman for this message, the thirteenth man speaks to the girl, who has penetrated into the domain of the taboo. The two taboo violators establish a bond so that the cursed domain—and along with it the father, who himself is a taboo violator—can be redeemed.

In the feminine psyche, the collective denial of evil and darkness in the male-determined realm of Christian culture must be discovered and dealt with as an already internalized norm. Otherwise the woman will be unable to come to terms with herself: within her, this masculine perspective rules the final inmost chamber. Within her, evil (and thus also the dark aspect of the feminine) is repressed, along with Judas. As long as the masculine element in her remains so stunted and shut out, it remains bewitched in the castle of the black woman, under the spell of the Great Mother, which it is unable to overcome so long as the dark aspect is split off. The girl is also incapable of overcoming it and remains in unconscious complicity with it as long as she has not discovered this taboo against evil and thus remains unable to come to grips with it.

The secret concealed in all the forbidden chambers in fairy

tales is the dark side, that which has been excluded by the prevailing patriarchal Christian culture. In all of these tales, compensatory, progressive forces of the collective unconscious are summoning liberating counterforces, for the most part feminine in nature, onto the scene. In order to get some overview of the range of these values denied by the prevailing culture, all we have to do, as the heroes and heroines of fairy tales do, is take a look in the forbidden room.[8]

There we find the split-off realm of nature, represented, for example, by the cage with three snakes, the green goose, or the green lizard. Also certainly to be included here is the raven, crucified, as it were, with three nails, who carried the princess off to the upper world on the world tree[9]—an inverted Christ analogue. The green maiden, half fish, half human, and the golden stag associated with her presumably embody the tabooed fascination with the erotic-sexual realm. The split-off feminine principle, especially in its chthonic form, appears in the figure of the black woman, or the witch. The dangerous devouring aspect of the Great Mother appears, for example, in the corpses that are hidden in the forbidden room. In addition, the all-too-bright Christian mother figure of Mary appears in her dark aspect, tabooed by the Christian consciousness, in "Mary the Cursed," who swings back and forth on a fiery swing and as she who, in "Mary's Child" (Grimm's no. 3) or its Russian variants, rips children from their mother's hands, sometimes even mutilating them, with incredible cruelty.

The womanly wisdom that is suppressed in our culture—the seeress' ability honored by the Germans and Celts, the frequent magical abilities of women—is compensatorily reflected in those tales in which, for example, four black maidens absorbed in their books appear in the forbidden room.

Finally, even men, deprived of their wholeness in this culture, appear in the tabooed room as in need of redemption. The animus figure needing to be saved is often identical with the future groom of the fairy tale heroine (this is the case in "Graycoat" and with the golden stag in the tale of the green maiden). From "Graycoat" to the thirteenth man in our tale stretches this inner connection, which occasionally is broadened from the presentation of a concrete animus figure to that of complex spiritual-religious contents, such as the Last Supper scene.

Profoundly interwoven with Western Christian culture and its taboos from the beginning is the biblical story of the Fall, which is itself one among many forbidden-tree tales. This tree confers knowledge that has been tabooed. This is what lured Eve, knowledge in threefold form, as it appears again in the tabooed room in the fairy tale: knowledge of good and evil, sexuality, and death. This is all synthesized in the snake's promise: "You will be like God, knowing good and evil." In my opinion, what is essentially at stake in all the temptation stories among the fairy tales is knowledge and integration, and our tale is exemplary in this respect.

The black woman now takes on characteristics of the devouring mother as we know them from the dark mother goddesses Kali and Durga. She herself kills the child—in another version by Gretchen Wild in Kassel,[10] it is the evil mother-in-law, but we hear nothing of her here—and, in order to cast suspicion on Goldilocks for killing the child, she smears Goldilocks's mouth with blood. In the other variant just mentioned, the queen is also sprayed with blood. There the queen is punished with muteness through a blow on the mouth "that made the blood gush forth." This motif of the evidence of murder left to inculpate the queen is also found in other versions. In the Russian tale "Maryushka," one of the child's little legs is even stuck in her mouth, as though she had eaten the child. In "Do You Confess?" bones are left behind. In "Graycoat," entrails are wound around her chair. However, everywhere else, the child is only abducted; the only other version of which I am aware in which the child is killed is in "The Silent Girl,"[12] which comes from Italy. Here the child is smashed against the wall. All these gruesome variants cast light on the black woman's cursed quality and her need for redemption. At the same time, these gruesome details underline the horror of the queen's loss and the steadfastness of her silence. It is as though in this phase the black woman fears for her sole dominance over the queen now that she has given birth to this masculine force, the prince. The queen is growing ever stronger in her autonomy and for this reason, the black woman shows her opposing power. The next year, the same thing happens when the queen, as though to reinforce her own feminine force, gives birth to a girl who, with her blond hair and the star on her forehead, also belongs entirely to the light principle. The black woman also kills and carries off this child after Goldilocks refuses to betray the secret of the dark men. This tale is unlike the variants in that a third child is not born. This is certainly because the primary focus is on the boy-girl pair, the masculine and feminine forces of the queen, which now enter upon an equal development.

But the suspicion of being a "devouring mother" finally falls on Goldilocks and everyone in the castle is "seized with horror." The king reacts in a more severe fashion here than in other variants ("In the House of the Black Woman," "Do You Confess?"), where he continues to try to protect his queen from the people. He himself commands "that the queen be burned in front of the castle." Thus the masculine king-component of the psyche issues the command to burn the woman, because her children, as symbols of future development, seem to be meeting misfortune on a regular basis. Just as the attainment of a certain wholeness seemed to be almost within reach, this image shows that the psyche is once again menaced by a deep split, for now the king-component turns against the queen. The queen is to be executed outside the castle. For the second time, she is cast out of the symbolic domain of wholeness.

THE TRANSFORMATION OF THE WHOLE

Now the smith's daughter is to be given over to the flames—notably enough, the element of a smith's handiwork. Those who burned witches in olden times were aware of the purificatory and transformational power of fire. According to the conceptions of those times, the "black" soul of the witch was purified by burning, an unmistakable parallel to the alchemical notion of its task.

Face to face with the stake, Goldilocks is once more interrogated by the black woman about what she saw in the hundredth room, but she maintains her silence. The fire is lit. "But as the flames approached her feet"—the sentence is formulated in this noticeably ambiguous fashion, so that it could almost be understood that at the same time the fire was approaching the feet of the black woman—"the black woman suddenly turned completely white." The fire's sudden proximity seems to have triggered something like a shock; a kind of transfiguration takes place. The black woman, having become white, suddenly assumes the intercessional role of the great Mary: "Put out the fire, put out the fire!" she cries. All of a sudden the significance of all the suffering the girl has borne as a result of her silence becomes clear: the transformation of the black woman, of the ambivalent Great Mother, from the nigredo to the albedo. The devouring mother again becomes the giving and providing mother. She brings the children back and now even becomes Goldilocks's defender and intercedes to save her life.

The most noticeable parallel at this point is found in the tale "In the House of the Black Woman," where the woman is discovered in the forbidden room in the throes of her transformation, which has reached every part of her except her toes. In that case, the redemptive process is connected with cleaning the castle, while in our tale it is more closely connected with exploration of the castle—in psychological terms, self-exploration—including the discovery of the room of the black men with its previously unconscious animus aspect. That the girl's work—remaining silent and suffering the consequences—is intimately bound up with the redemption of the black woman is stated, among the variants known to me, only by the Italian one, "The Silent Girl"; in that tale, a death spirit, who in her lifetime was an evil, domineering woman, is to be liberated from her penitential torment. And indeed the green maiden, who is seen by the girl "in her distress," is ultimately redeemed by the silent solidarity of the girl.

This point is quite different in "Do You Confess?," which is otherwise quite similar to our tale. There, it is not a woman in transformation that is discovered in the hundredth room, but a killer. And though here the girl is freed at the end from the black woman, who simply leaves her in peace, we hear nothing of a transformation of the black woman herself.

In "Graycoat," the cursed man is liberated by the girl at the end. Our story treats both motifs simultaneously: the dark aspects of the masculine and the feminine are both redeemed together by Goldilocks. Her ability to maintain through her silence the right balance of solidarity and distance in relation to the two archetypal powers makes possible the needed transformation.

Goldilocks finally redeems the psychic energy bound up in the dangerous, devouring aspect of the black woman, establishing her independence through her complicity in keeping the secret of the black men. That the dark aspect of the masculine principle has also been redeemed at the same time may be concluded from the king's boundless joy at the end of the story, which causes him to have the smith, his wife, and all his children brought to the court to stay for the rest of their days.

NOTES

1. In *Slawische Märchen*, translated by Werner Dausin (Hanau/Main, 1975).

2. *Märchen aus dem Donaulande* (Jena, 1926), pp. 29ff. Relating to this, cf. the interpretation of Marie-Louise von Franz, "Bei der Schwarzen Frau," in Laiblin (ed.), *Märchenforschung und Tiefenpsychologie: Wege der Forschung*, vol. C II (Darmstadt: Wissenschaftliche Buchgesellschaft, 1975).

3. "Die Grüne Jungfer" (The Green Maiden) in August Ey, *Harzmärchen oder Sagen und Märchen aus dem Oberharz* (Stade, 1862), pp. 176ff.

4. "Das verschwiegene Mädchen" (The Silent Girl) in "Märchen der europäischen Völker," unpublished manuscript, edited by Karl Schulte-Kemminghausen and Georg Hülle, yearly proceedings for 1963 of the Gesellschaft zur Pflege des Märchenkultus der Europäischen Völker e. V. (Westphalia: Aschendorff/Münster, 1963) pp. 159ff.

5. Cf. J. Bolte and G. Polivka, *Anmerkungen zu den Kinder- und Hausmärchen der Brüder Grimm*, vol. 1 (Leipzig, 1913), pp. 13ff.

6. Jean Chevalier and Alain Gheerbrant (eds.), *Dictionnaire des symboles* (Paris: Éditions Robert Laffont, 1969), article on number thirteen, pp. 964–965.

7. Cited in ibid. Cf. also Bolte and Polivka, *Anmerkungen*, commentary 5.

8. Cf. Bolte and Polivka, *Anmerkungen*, commentary 5.

9. "Die Prinzessin auf dem Baum," *Deutsche Märchen seit Grimm* (1912), pp. 1ff. Also in relation to this, cf. C. G. Jung, *Bewußtes und Unbewußtes* (The Conscious and the Unconscious) (Frankfurt: Fischer-Taschenbuch, 1957) pp. 92ff.

10. Cf. Bolte and Polivka, *Anmerkungen*, commentary 5.

11. "Das verschwiegene Mädchen" (see note 4).

PART THREE

Fairy Tale Motifs in Psychotherapy

MARIO JACOBY

Bewitchment and Liberation

Working Therapeutically with Fairy Tale Motifs

In the dreams, complexes, and behavior patterns of analysands, archetypal constellations come into view, including those relating to darkness and evil, that we are familiar with from parallels in fairy tales; the meanings and potentialities for transformation of these archetypes can be derived from the corresponding fairy· tales. When fairy tale motifs such as the mortally dangerous unapproachability of the riddle-posing Princess Turandot, the sleep curse of Sleeping Beauty ("Brier Rose," Grimm's no. 50) or the secret knowledge of the griffin (Grimm's no. 165) arise spontaneously in dreams or in the archetypally influenced transference patterns of analysands, we are able to draw conclusions about therapeutic possibilities from the denouements of pertinent fairy tales.

One of my patients was in the habit of criticizing all the comments and interpretations I came up with during our sessions. According to her, it was of no value to recount dreams to me or write them up, since I did not understand them anyhow and was a dreadful dream interpreter. Analysis with me was valueless altogether, and she was considering not coming back. Nonetheless, she always came back.

As an analyst, one must often put up with this sort of thing. The idea that one is always and exclusively loved and honored by one's patients is hardly accurate. It is of course extremely important at such times for the analyst to ask himself, without overly undermining his confidence, if and to what extent he really is failing to understand his patients. In the case under discussion, however, one thing became quite clear: the patient discredited not only nearly everything that came from me, but also her own thoughts, ideas, and impulses. She was stuck in the middle of a university dissertation, which was driving her to despair. She felt completely blocked.

Every thought that came to her was discredited the moment she tried to put it on paper. "But that makes no sense, it's too superficial, it's not exactly what I wanted to say"—this kind of instant criticism was incapacitating and discouraging her. Destructive criticism of herself and persons closely related to her had become almost an autonomous mechanism that she was unable to guide and control. Through the analysis, she came to the insight that she was really very frightened of these tendencies toward discreditation. After some time, she was able to tell me that she was continually plagued by the fear of having to discredit and criticize me, to accuse me of not understanding her. At this point, an interpretation spontaneously came to mind, which I formulated to her in this way: "Your problem seems to be similar to that of Princess Turandot or the Princess in the Norwegian tale 'The Companion.' [See Verena Kast's detailed interpretation of the parallel tale "The Cursed Princess" in Part Two.] They had to set their suitors unsolvable riddles in order to destroy them when they failed to come up with the solutions. You are keeping yourself unapproachable in the same way. And yet deep down, you want to be redeemed." The story of Turandot was familiar to my analysand; she read the Norwegian fairy tale the same evening.

As emerges from my characterization, my analysand was indeed putting forth a great deal of effort to make herself unapproachable. Anything that signaled "dangerous" closeness had to be done in. This included her own ideas, her needs for intimacy, and, among other things, my interpretations. This can be a very difficult therapeutic problem, one that is only inadequately formulated in the technical term *resistance*. In fairy tales in which princesses pose unsolvable riddles, often there is a demonic father figure in the background who will not relinquish the princess to her suitors. In "The Companion,"[1] the princess is the beloved of a troll, a mountain spirit. As a last trial, she sets her suitor the task of bringing her the next morning whatever it is she is thinking of. The hero succeeds, with the help of his companion who has magical powers, presenting her with the head of the troll, which is what she had thought of. Though she now marries, the danger is not overcome until the princess is entirely divested of her troll skin.

This difficult problem was also constellated in my patient. What had to be done was to determine what "spirit" possessed her so as to be able to "cut off its head"—to render it partially inoperative. The moment she was able to talk to me about her fear of having to discredit me and all persons closely related to her, she was no longer totally identified with this spirit. Thus we were able to seek the solution of this spirit's riddle together. It was a spirit that wanted her to keep far away from everything human and having to do with human life. "I smell human flesh," such a spirit says menacingly. The bad part was that it was primarily her own humanity that she was unable to live and experience. To live in a body means to be enclosed in one's skin, not to be able to get out of one's skin. It sweats and it stinks, and the most pleasurable bodily needs are at the same time disgusting and embarrassing. Being human involves the experience of limitedness, imperfection, the necessity of compromise—the experience of the shadow. My analysand was always convinced that nothing in herself and her life was right or suitable. She could not affirm or accept anything about herself. Fundamentally, mediocrity, limitation, and compromise were unbearable for her. There was a spirit in her that demanded omniscience and omnipotence, that trod on the human worm that she felt herself to be, seeking mercilessly to completely trample it underfoot. Thus she had to remain aloof from humanity in its true sense. Getting into human involvements meant being trampled down; writing an imperfect dissertation became impossible, because it was nothing but human.

There are technical terms for this condition as well, depending on the models of the different psychotherapeutic schools. In Jungian psychology, we would speak of animus possession; in the psychoanalytic narcissism theory of Heinz Kohut, it would be fixation on the grandiose self of early childhood. We also speak of schizoid personalities with their fear of human proximity. The most graphic and empathic description of the analysand's condition, however, was the fairy tale, which even triggered a half-acknowledging "Aha!" reaction in my patient.

Now it must be said that this fairy tale example was not derived directly from the dreams or fantasies of the patient but spontaneously occurred to me, the therapist. I experienced the patient as someone who had been captured by a father/mountain spirit. Nonetheless, the main point here is that it seemed to provide the best image for the situation of the patient, and it was meaningful to her. It helped her, as well as me, to gain a better grasp of her problem, which was an important step in the therapy. The basic pattern of her style of experiencing—the archetypal thematic—became visible; now this had to be worked through further within the context of her personal life history. Fairy tale motifs can thus be of significant help to the therapist in formulating interpretations; this is what I wanted to show here.

Let us now turn our attention to examples of fairy tale motifs in patients' material.

A twenty-seven-year-old man recounted the following dream to me after about nine months of analysis:

> I am going up into the forest. Snow-covered meadows lead to it. In the forest itself, there is no further path. I am wearing my bathrobe, and suddenly I see my mother coming, also wearing her bathrobe. Together we go down a path and

come to a house. There in the back room, my girlfriend is sleeping. I go through all the rooms until I find her, give her a kiss, and she wakes up.

The sleeping princess, Brier Rose or Sleeping Beauty, is awakened with a kiss in this dream—or does this interpretation seem too forced? The young man undertook analysis because, as he said, he could not decide whether or not to marry his girlfriend. He could not give her up and he would not marry her. For her part, the girlfriend demanded that they get engaged. This conflict was giving him a hard time and had mobilized visible fears. It became clear to me rather quickly that the young man was not able to commit himself to anything. He gave the impression of being asleep. There was hardly anything that could stir his emotions.

As the dream shows, though he had a girlfriend, she slept in the back room; she did not sleep with him. In reality, the girlfriend seemed to be rather active and demanding. For him, though, she was sleeping, alone, in the back room. That is the way the situation appears in him, in his way of experiencing it. Thus something in him must first be awakened in order for him to become receptive toward the feelings and emotions that constitute any engagement or commitment. The expression "to become receptive" just happened to occur to me, but it seems to be accurate. What is sleeping in him is his receptivity, which is regarded as being specifically feminine. C. G. Jung, as we know, spoke of "mistress soul," the anima of the man, which is symbolized in feminine form. The anima can also be called the archetype of life. To be "animated" means to feel emotionally alive.

Just the opposite was the case with my patient. He felt tired and incapacitated. The curse of his life, he frequently repeated, was that he had lost his father when he was only eight years old. (If we think of Sleeping Beauty, her sleep was also brought about by a fateful curse, by a fate-determining fairy.) After the death of his father, left with his mother and two older sisters, he was the only male member of the family. His reaction to the death of his father and the domination of the women was to go on a speech strike. He hardly spoke anymore; he closed himself off, encapsulated himself. The mother did everything to stop her son from spinning this cocoon around himself: kindly encouragement, threats, and blows followed by further cheering-up. (In the fairy tale, all the spindles in the entire kingdom had to be burned, because after the curse of the evil fairy, spinning was regarded as dangerous.) From that point on, the boy adopted a posture of submissiveness toward his mother, his family, and the other people around him. Only in the "upstairs room" did he continue his secret spinning—in the room of the old woman.[2] The autonomous fantasies that continued behind the door locked with the rusty key expressed both his longing for omnipotence and his destructive fears. Thus the analysand reported that he was compelled to occupy himself with a desire to be everywhere in the whole world at the same time. He did not want anybody to be experiencing anything anywhere without his being there. Therefore he was really always restless. Particularly, when he heard an airplane, he wanted to be on it. A yearning to fly overseas would then take hold of him. He in fact did fly overseas, but that gave him no satisfaction. For once he was there, he was still once again just in *one* place and not present at events taking place elsewhere. Therefore he preferred to go to sleep, because then he was not subject to this kind of restlessness.

Even when his emotionality and vitality—his anima—seemed to be asleep, he was spinning these webs of irreality continually, with ongoing repetitiveness. That is why the old woman upstairs, spinning in the tower, is such an appropriate symbol. His sense of engagement with life has been pricked on this spindle. When he was with his girlfriend, he was assailed by doubts about her being the right one for him. If he were to commit himself to her, as he thought of it, it would mean passing up thousands of opportunities to meet a more suitable woman. However, he was far too passive to pursue these thousands of opportunities in any concrete way. All that remained mere sterile fantasy, which did not help in the slightest to answer the question of whether his girlfriend was really the right partner for him. I must add that my patient was not in the least "crazy" in the psychotic sense. It was clear to him that he was dealing with unactualizable fantasies, and he wanted to counter this through analysis.

When we look at his dream, in the upper levels we find, not the tower room with the old woman, but instead a snow-covered forest where there is no path. In reality, my patient's defense against what he experienced as inner emptiness consisted primarily of indulging himself in "wise thoughts" that viewed life from a commanding distance, of being high above things on the mountain, assuming a superior vantage point. If he could not be lively, he wanted at least to be wise. In this way he unconsciously sought to maintain his self-esteem. The dream shows that he takes his bathrobe up there with him. That he nevertheless is frozen inside is also clearly evident from the dream, as is the fact that the way up leads no further. Now it is his mother, also in her bathrobe, who brings him down from there and takes him to his girlfriend's house. It certainly would not be farfetched at this point to think of incestuous Oedipal fantasies. What strikes us, however, is that the mother is very closely allied with him because she too is wearing a bathrobe; this contrasts with his experience of his actual mother. In reality, his mother was a rather hysterical person who was continually trying to control her environment through hyperactivity; she was moody and reproachful toward him. Thus in the dream the mother underwent a change. This points to a change in his inner mother image—according to the dream, a favorable change, for after all, she leads him to his girlfriend's house.

Experience shows that a change in parental images occurs in analysis to a great extent through the experiences we call transference. When we talk about transference, we are referring to the fact that many patients carry their early experiences and conflicts with regard to their parents and siblings around inside them as an unconscious vision of the world, and this vision is reactivated in the relationship with the analyst. At the same time, they may also seek from the analyst whatever was missing in the way of parental affection and empathy; this missing affection has usually played a role in the development of the person's psychological disturbance. Normally, one would imagine that now my patient would seek in me his prematurely deceased father. In fact he actually chose a male analyst because he saw in the loss of his father his greatest deficiency. Certainly a great deal passed between us on this level. Nevertheless, it was not his father who awakened his anima-soul but his mother. There is no doubt that his mother was even more profoundly constellated between us. I tried wherever possible to take my cue from him, to attune myself to his rhythm and his rather monotonous melody. As much as possible, I refrained from being demanding or disapproving or exaggeratedly encouraging as his own mother had been, even though his sleepiness tended to provoke such reactions.

This kind of feeling attunement was a new experience for him. It corresponded archetypally to the maternal attitude of empathy and care. The archetypal kindly mother is symbolized in the Sleeping Beauty tale by the good fairies, all of whom are concerned that their protégée be able to have a rich and full life. Ultimately, they represent nature and its psychophysical ripening processes seeking to come to fruition. The gifts, that is, our natural endowments and talents, ought to be able to unfold in a natural manner—and the capacity for love as well. That is human nature's urge.

In any case, a year later, my analysand was able to marry his girlfriend and later become a father. From time to time, he has minor relapses when the old woman in the tower begins to spin again and his inner aliveness goes back to sleep. On the whole, however, his sense of engagement in life has been awakened.

Let us turn now to another dream, that of a forty-five-year-old artistically talented woman. She had undertaken a course of study at a university and had to earn her livelihood at the same time. At the time of the dream, she was busy writing a paper to fulfill the requirements of one of her professors and thus had an overfull workload to cope with. This was the dream:

> "I am in a round, glass-enclosed space. A professor comes in who tells me that he has taught two birds how to talk. He takes one of the birds around the glass pavilion. I hear, somewhat unclearly, that it is speaking. This bird looks like a Japanese or Korean man and is wearing a swallowtail cutaway. It has yellowish-colored skin and is speaking German in a rather rapid, parrotlike fashion. The same thing happens with the second bird. I have the somewhat strange feeling of being in the griffin's house. But I admire the professor. At least he had achieved something with the birds. One of the bird-men says to me: "Was I somewhat unclear? Well, that will improve."

So the analysand dreamed she was in the griffin's house. She knew the Swiss-German version of the fairy tale that is part of the Grimm's collection (no. 165). In this fairy tale the griffin is described both as omniscient and as a devourer of Christians. "No Christian can speak with the bird, he eats them all up." The whole fairy tale, including many of the details, is a variant of the other Grimm's story "The Devil with the Three Golden Hairs" (no. 29). Mythologically, the griffin is a mixed form. It has an eagle's head and a lionlike body, four feet, and two powerful wings. It is a magical beast, capable of drawing a chariot through the air. Thus, like the phoenix, it is connected with the symbolism of the sun. It also guards treasures of gold, and magic can be performed with a feather from its tail. Originally, the griffin was a hybrid creature from the ancient Near East. Depictions of it from Babylon, Egypt, and the Mycenaean culture are extant.[3] In the Grimm's tale, the king gives the hero the task of fetching a feather from the griffin's tail. If he succeeds in this feat, he is to receive the king's daughter for his wife. A similar task is set for the hero in "The Devil with the Three Golden Hairs." There, in order to get the king's daughter, three golden hairs have to be pulled out of the devil's head. Now, it is interesting that in both tales it is not only the feather or the devil's golden hairs that are important but also the knowledge connected with them. In "The Devil with the Three Golden Hairs," the devil *knows* why the marketplace fountain, out of which wine used to flow, has dried up and does not provide even water anymore, why the tree that once bore golden apples does not even leaf anymore, and so forth. There is a toad under a stone in the fountain that has to be killed; a mouse is gnawing on the root of the tree, that is why it is withering. In the griffin version, the bird knows why the king's daughter is incurably ill—a toad has made a nest from her hair. Of all beings, it is the Christian-devouring griffin and the devil who possess the knowledge of why things in the world go sterile and sick. But what does that mean? To do justice to this theme from a psychological point of view, an entire cultural history would have to be written. Nonetheless, what we can say is that Christianity—especially since its fusion with the Neoplatonic tradition during the history of the early church—brought with it a pronounced devaluation of nature and of the natural in man. Since the teachings of Saint Augustine, original sin has been strongly associated with sexuality. Paul believed chastity was more pleasing to God than marrying. To be "carnally" minded is an act of opposition to God, or death (Rom. 8:5, 6). The opposition between spirit and nature was loaded in favor of spirit. The Near Eastern fertility cults, in which magical-sexual practices were carried out with prostitutes sacred to Astarte or Ishtar, were already an offense to Judaism and its God—thus the eternal struggle of the Old Testament prophet against the cult of Baal. Baal was a vegetation god who, with nature, died and was resurrected. He was also venerated in the form of a bull or a boar. The pig as a fertility symbol was also part of his sphere; that is why the pig is an impure animal for the Jews.[4] Moreover, the devil was often represented with goat's feet and horns, a mixture of ancient nature-god forms. The natural, instinctive element, which for ancient men was a gift from the gods, became for Christians evil and ungodly. Thus man, who is begotten and born through natural means, is primordially tainted by original sin, is by his very nature sinful and evil. Medieval education in monastic schools went so far as to beat the devil out of children as much as possible.[5] Even the educational method devised by August Hermann Francke in the eighteenth century on religio-pietistic principles is based on the idea that children must continually be watched and punished—if left to themselves, they just do evil. The "natural stubbornness" of the child has to be broken and must be replaced by genuine Christian humility—in other words, obedience. Children's games are mere idleness and represent for a child a lure of the "worldly spirit."[6]

The devil or the griffin is thus primarily an image of the discredited natural drives and instincts that have been repressed into the unconscious. One has to avoid them because otherwise the Christian is devoured. Thus this kind of whitewashed Christianity is continually in danger of being overrun by compensatory natural drives. The history of Christianity is full of examples—heretic burnings and the Inquisition gave the aggressions almost a perversely free rein, and witch trials did the same for the sexual drive with its fantasies. Very probably, this kind of *opus contra naturam* ("work against nature") was initially necessary for Christianity to attain its due level of spirituality. However, with time this sort of one-sided endeavor became sterile—not least because it seems to conflict with the psychic striving for wholeness and tends to force psychic transformation into a predetermined track. The Renaissance was already an attempt to regain the ancient joy in life and nature. Attempts to compensate for traditional Christianity from the philosophical side have become numerous in modern times. We have only to recall Rousseau, who declared that man was by nature good and therefore should be left as much as possible to his own nature and to nature in the world around him. Nietzsche wanted to reawaken Dionysos, who after all is intimately linked to the devil; and for Klages, the mind became the antagonist of the soul.

Modern psychotherapy is based to a great extent on the view, depicted in the fairy tale, that the Christian-devouring griffin or devil possesses a knowledge that can supply a wealth of help against mental and psychic sterility. What is it that Freudian psychoanalysis tries to do? It tries to do away with the repression of the instinctual drives and subordinate them to the free access of consciousness. "Where id was, there ego shall be," says Freud.[7] Out of the sterility of neurotic fragmentation, the ability to love, work, and enjoy life should arise through the accessibility of the drives and instincts. Jungian psychology seeks to do away with the dissociation from the unconscious as well. But according to Jung, the unconscious is made up not only of repressions and instinctual drives connected with one's personal life history, but also of highly meaningful psychic potentialities called archetypes. For him, the instincts contain both the germ of spiritual development and the potential for creative ideation. In a certain way, the unconscious knows more than consciousness. With this, we come to the paradox of "unconscious knowledge." There must be other knowledge beyond our conscious knowledge. The whole, extremely complex physiology of the human body "knows" how to function in a life-maintaining fashion. It knew that long before human knowledge in the form of science was able to observe and investigate these processes and their laws. The stomach seems to know when it needs to be filled and communicates this to us in the form of hunger. The sex drive knows how to affect us, otherwise humanity would have died out long ago. Even human consciousness and our ability to reflect is something that has been appropriately included in our makeup in a species-specific fashion. Thus there must be a knowledge in nature that equipped humans

with the potential for consciousness in the first place. Our capacity for consciousness is thus a natural phenomenon, the manifestation of a knowledge in nature. Biblical mythology affirms
this by saying that God made man in His own image. I have
already suggested why in our fairy tale this knowledge of the unconscious is symbolized by the devil or the Christian-devouring
griffin. When we have exhausted our conscious approach, when
everything—our whole life, our thoughts and feelings—seems
hollow and lifeless or we are plagued by depression or other symptoms, then we turn to the unconscious and its manifestations—
dreams, for example—in order to find out what is gnawing on the
roots of our life, or where some toad has obstructed life's flow.
We look for a way back to our nature. Instead of fleeing from our
inner difficulties in one way or another—through empty busy-
ness, pleasure-seeking, physical ailments, and so on—we attempt
to make ourselves available for the confrontation with the inner
devil. That which seems to us most immoral, mean, and disgusting, which for the most part we evaluate as such from the point
of view of a narrow conscious perspective, is precisely what we
must acknowledge in ourselves. This is the devil as unlived or
repressed life. But it is interesting that in both tales the confrontation with the griffin or devil does not take a direct form. The
devil has a grandmother who takes pity on the hero, and the griffin has a wife. Both hide the hero and use their cunning with the
devil and the griffin. These female figures correspond in turn to
the fact that the unconscious as Mother Nature appears in the
first instance as feminine; symbolically, it takes on the form of the
Great Mother. The devil or the griffin is then the spiritual aspect
inherent in the natural-vegetative realm, that is, the spirit in
nature, instinctive natural knowledge.

Having made this amplificatory digression, let us return to
the dream. Though the dreamer has the feeling of being in the
griffin's house, the situation nevertheless looks fundamentally different. Instead of the grandmother delousing the devil, we have

the professor training the bird. The birds are humanized even though they look foreign and they speak German in a parrotlike fashion. The professor's trick is thus highly questionable—he is trying to train the autonomous life out of the unconscious. It is also significant that the whole event is taking place in a glass pavilion. Though life going on around can be seen and considered through the glass, at the same time one is separated from it. The dream seems to be an ironic variation on the fairy tale known to the analysand. It shows her the parrotlike sterility she was being driven toward by her exaggerated admiration for the professor, that is, by her intellectual ambitions, overblown at the expense of what is alive in her. It becomes evident that she was demanding too much from herself in the way of training and thus has come into conflict with her own nature and inner depth. Her behavior could not have been brought to consciousness better than through the irony of this dream. It was therefore necessary to talk about the psychological meaning of the fairy tale of the griffin much as I have done above. In this way I was able to point out to her the discrepancy between her dream and the fairy tale as graphically as possible. It is always astounding to see how accurately our inner natural knowledge is able to make itself heard. On the instinctive level, our dreamer seemed to know what was good for the psychological balance of her personality. On that basis, her one-sided behavior was accurately highlighted through irony. Jung, as is well known, held the view that dreams exercise a compensatory function in maintaining our psychic balance. This dream is a good example of such a view.

I have tried to provide some examples of how fairy tales can play an important role in psychotherapeutic practice. Rather than painstakingly interpreting individual fairy tales, I have tried to illuminate certain motifs that arose in therapeutic practice. The question remains whether and to what extent an approach of this type is legitimate. Do we not do violence to the fairy tale by trying to see it as a model for the resolution of conflicts? Is this not a *déformation professionelle?* Is it admissible suddenly to see the beautiful Sleeping Beauty as a personality component of my sleepy analysand rather than as the inhabitant of a marvelous fairy tale castle?

Fairy tales, as the product of human imagination, are also self-representations of the psyche and its processes. Thus psychological interpretation of fairy tales more or less imposes itself, especially since Jung with his hypotheses concerning the archetypes of the collective unconscious has provided us with a decisive key for their interpretation. In my view, dealing with fairy tales psychologically brings both a gain and a loss. The gain is obviously that it makes it possible to experience heretofore unconscious factors. As long as Sleeping Beauty remains in her royal castle, is blessed and cursed, lives and falls asleep there, she remains embedded in her own world. She has a fixed place in our imagination, which might remind us of our childhood when our mother told us the story or when we might have seen it sentimentally presented as a children's play, perhaps as a Christmas story. On the other hand, Sleeping Beauty as a symbol of our own sleepiness and lifelessness is something that, under certain circumstances, we might experience very directly and immediately. Nonetheless, it always seems to me that with this approach a certain loss must also be reckoned with. This is a loss of poetry, of the special atmosphere of the fairy tale world. In my view, we should properly speak of a *déformation professionelle* if in working with fairy tales psychologically, we lose our naive openness toward their miraculous poetry. However, in reality, such a lamentable loss can occur with or without psychology.

NOTES

1. "Der Kamarad" (The Companion), in *Norwegisches Volksmärchen*, Märchen der Weltliteratur, no. 27 (Diederichs, 1967).
2. In the fairy tale "Brier Rose" (Grimm's no. 50), the curse of the evil

fairy was to fall due on Brier Rose's fifteenth birthday, when she was to prick her finger on a spindle and fall down dead. But the twelfth good fairy, who had saved her wish for last, commuted the curse to one of a hundred years' sleep. On Brier Rose's fifteenth birthday, "the king and queen happened to be away from home and she was left all alone. She went all over the castle, examining room after room, and finally she came to an old tower. She climbed the narrow winding staircase, which led to a little door with a rusty key in the lock. She turned the key, the door sprang open, and there in a small room sat an old woman with a spindle, busily spinning her flax." Brier Rose pricks her finger on the old woman's spindle, and she and all the castle fall under the curse of a hundred years' sleep. (*Grimm's Tales for Young and Old*, translated by Ralph Manheim (Garden City, N.Y.: Doubleday & Company, Inc., 1977), pp. 175ff.)—Translator

3. H. Bächtold-Stäubli, "Greif," in *Handwörterbuch des deutschen Aberglaubens* (Berlin: de Gruyter, 1930/31).
4. V. Maag, "Syrien-Palästina," in Schmökel, *Kulturgeschichte des alten Orients* (Stuttgart: Kröner, 1961), pp. 595ff.
5. H. Reble, *Geschichte der Pädagogik* (Stuttgart: Klett, 1962), pp. 44ff.
6. Ibid., p. 117.
7. Sigmund Freud, *The Standard Edition of the Complete Psychological Works of Sigmund Freud*, edited and translated by James Strachey (London: Hogarth, 1957), vol. 22, p. 208.

MARIO JACOBY

Sleeping Beauty and
The Evil Fairy
On the Problem of Excluded Evil

A *case of teenage anorexia shows what the Sleeping Beauty ("Brier Rose," Grimm's no. 50) constellation can mean in the psychological problems of a young girl. As we see, it can even bring about the failure of psychotherapeutic treatment (which also gets caught in the brier hedge). The reflection of the Sleeping Beauty problem in transference and counter-transference particularly deserves our attention.*

As has already been made clear, every fairy tale, either openly or in a more hidden way, presents some deficiency or crisis at the beginning. An unsatisfactory state of affairs is described, which can be interpreted psychologically as suffering. As is well known, though suffering can have a crippling effect, at the same time, without the suffering resulting from conflicts and crises, the development of consciousness and maturation are unthinkable. Suffering is one of the most important sources of energy triggering the development of consciousness. The question of the meaning of life ultimately arises from painful conflicts. The best and most valuable creative achievements—whether spiritual, scientific, or artistic in nature—are founded in the vulnerability of human existence to the experience of suffering.[1]

Thus for the psychological understanding of fairy tales, it is always important to inquire into the significance of the initial crisis. Fairy tales always describe fantasized possibilities of release and liberation from crises and conflicts that are typically inherent in human experience. In "Sleeping Beauty," this crisis is constituted by the fact that the king and queen are unable to have a child. The situation is barren. Symbolically, childlessness signifies that the renewal of life cannot take place. The living psychic process is obstructed, which usually brings a fundamental feeling of emptiness, boredom, and unbearable meaninglessness. It is just this fundamental feeling that, among other factors, motivates many people to undergo psychotherapy and that constitutes the "pressure of suffering" necessary to bring them to this decision.

In order to understand the beginning of this tale more precisely, we have to look into the meaning of "king" and "queen." Like all fairy tale figures, they are not to be conceived of as individual persons but as symbol bearers who possess a certain value and status in the action as a whole. Some essential factors for a psychological understanding of "king" have already been discussed (see the first chapter, "C. G. Jung's View of Fairy Tale Interpretation"). The king symbolizes the dominant worldview and its system of values. Thus he represents a norm, an apparently sacrosanct guiding image that provides a reference point for human behavior. Originally, the king was considered an embodiment of divine power on earth. The norms he embodies thus categorically possess a living, culture-shaping significance. As already mentioned, however, as soon as innovations of a religious, philosophical, or political nature become established, organized, and institutionalized, they lose their immediacy, their living impact. Let us take as an example the spontaneity of religious experience in early Christianity. This was a religious departure that inspired a new sense of the meaning of life and exercised a vital inner power of persuasion that could not be shaken even by martyrdom and death. With time, the original experience of individuals became an institution; Christianity was proclaimed a state religion. This was a great victory, but at the same time a decisive loss. The kingdom of Christ, which is "not of this world," was incorporated into the power structure precisely of "this world" and divested of many of its dimensions—to say nothing of the perversion and abuse it was then exposed to. Already in the first centuries, synods spelled out which religious concepts and ideas were Christian and which were not. On the one hand, this was surely necessary; on the other hand, authoritative doctrinal norms developed out of this process that increasingly claimed to be absolute. In this way, an ancient Christian principle was given up—the appeal to the illumination bestowed upon the individual by the Holy Ghost. Dogmatism arose, fixation of a system of philosophical, legal, and political safeguards, which still today may not be called into question. At its apex is the pope, who to a great extent embodies the king in this sphere. Then Luther once again took the "word of God" as proclaimed in the Gospels—the "Good News"—as an immediate source of inspiration. A direct meeting between the individual and God, the inner experience of the "word of God," was the renewed concern of nascent Protestantism. But this new, highly significant, radical religious resurgence soon rigidified into national churches and the orthodox Heidelberg catechism. The "king" became sterile.

Such a course of events corresponds to archetypal laws. Life, in its psychic and spiritual as well as its biological aspects, requires constant renewal.

Today, for the most part, "kings"—established values—are constantly being dethroned. But unexpectedly, out of nowhere, we find that there is already a new "king" on the throne. For example, for the last decade[2] we have been hearing the call for anti-authoritarian education, for freedom from repression by the Establishment, for a revolution in the existing unjust social order. But what authoritarian "kings" we find surreptitiously establishing themselves through this process! What fanatical intolerance these ideas of anti-authoritarianism, social justice, and freedom, though valuable in themselves, bring to bear on those caught in their grip!

It is important to dethrone kings. However, the symbolic content of the notion of "king" cannot be set aside, because it is a component of human nature. Nonetheless we must not let the inner king rule in an unrestricted and authoritarian fashion—which he is always able to do when we are unconscious of his rule, when we fail to call our dominant inner values into question. In this way, we are degraded to the level of mere subjects, mere instruments of collective norms. Many people cannot tolerate this subject condition for long, since it tends to produce neurosis, to obstruct the process of individuation. For this reason, therapeutic analysis consists in large part of rendering conscious and thus modifying dominant inner values that have become destructive, revealing the inner king in his character and action. This problem is often portrayed in fairy tales as the renewal of the king.

What does "queen" mean? The queen is the feminine antithesis within a value system dominated by the king. In contrast to the king, the son of the sun,[3] as the feminine principle she is associated with the moon.[4] For instance, in Mozart's *Magic Flute*, we have the Queen of the Night. As a nocturnal heavenly light, the moon cannot bring out full brilliance and full color. It illuminates with a silvery luster and stirs intuition. The most beautiful lyrical poetry is inspired by the moon and its unique magic. Sunlight enables clear delimitation of individual objects; it stands for diurnal wakefulness and clarity of consciousness. Moonlight evokes for the most part particular moods: longing, delight, devotion, or sadness. Thus, while the king represents the clearly delimited norm of the prevailing worldview with its attendant values, the queen signifies an intuitive sensibility for hidden moods and feelings, an openness toward the unconscious and irrational. She is something like the weak spot within the royal system, but one that repeatedly reveals itself in fairy tales as pregnant with the future. Only the feminine principle can bear something new, because of its receptivity and its closeness to nature and the psyche.

But in our tale, the royal couple is barren. Their relationship is not fruitful. Something in the natural process is disturbed. Then, typically, it is the queen who undertakes an action that confronts the crisis. She gets into the bath.

The bath and immersion in the bath have an extremely rich symbolism. In ancient Greece, before every rite in the mysteries, a bath had to be taken. In ancient times, on Yom Kippur, the Jewish Day of Atonement, the high priest had to bathe himself entirely five times and wash his hands and feet ten times. The Christian baptism was originally a total immersion in water; in the Greek Orthodox Church, newborn children are still fully submerged in water at baptism. "The king and queen bathing" plays a major role in alchemistic symbolism, much of which is described by Jung.[5] Bathing obviously has to do with *purificatio*, outer and inner purification. At the same time, as can be seen from baptism and the mystery cults, it prepares the way for a deeper process of transformation. In fairy tales, bathing is frequently present as a redemption motif. Through bathing, characters who have been changed into animals often regain their real human form. Water, as an absolutely indispensable primal element of life, is a symbol for the creative unconscious. Coming in contact with water or being immersed in water also means being washed over by this element, entering into relation with the living element in oneself.

This is what the queen in our fairy tale does. Psychologically, we can take this as meaning that she fully faces her situation, taking seriously all the feelings, fantasies, and associations grouped around the "being empty and sterile" complex. This could have a purificatory and psychocathartic effect. In any case, the bath sets a process in motion.

In the story, next comes the prompt appearance of the frog, who climbs out of the water to announce the birth of a girl. It is impossible to suppress the heretical thought that here we have a curious variation on the Annunciation in the New Testament. To the Virgin Mary the angel of the Lord appears; in our fairy tale, there appears a frog. Let us try with the help of amplification to understand what the frog might mean psychologically in this context. Frogs are especially conspicuous for their naked skin, which absorbs moisture and at the same time secretes mucus. On account of this, they often evoke disgust in people. They are always found in the vicinity of water. Their life begins in the evening at twilight. In medieval times, frogs were used in love spells. They symbolize fertility and sexuality. The call of frogs in spring is associated in superstition with the screaming of unborn children.[6] Thus, psychologically, frogs have the quality of symbolizing contents strongly connected with birth, that is development of consciousness.[7] In contrast to the angel of the Lord, who belongs to the light-bathed realm of heaven, the frog is a primitive creature of the swamp and the night. At best, it is the dark Great Mother of nature who speaks through him,[8] who, in spite of light-oriented Christianity, claims her place in superstition, in the human psyche, and also in fairy tales. We could speculate that the sterility of the royal state of consciousness had something to do with the severe norms of Christianity, which were unfriendly to nature and one-sidedly spiritual. In the fairy tale, this would suggest compensation by the dark instinctual forces of nature. After all, fairy tales, with their magic- and superstition-related contents, are not Christian, but rather compensate for the official Christian orientation of consciousness. Thus from Great Mother Nature's dark realm of vital forces arises the new content, the heroine of our fairy tale.

The royal joy over the beautiful girl is great, and the wise women, the fairies, are invited to the feast. Here again, a deficiency of the kingdom is indicated: there are only twelve golden plates, so one of the thirteen wise women has to stay home. From this arises a threat to the newborn child. A threat to a child hero is a widespread mythological motif. The child Moses is abandoned to the river, the baby Zeus must be hidden from his devouring father Kronos, and so on. From the psychological standpoint, one is struck by the fact that contents manifesting in a nascent state are threatened by the old attitude. A glaring example of this is found in abating depressions, when a new feeling for life begins to appear. In this period, the patient must be watched most closely, since experience shows that at this point the danger of suicide is greatest.

To understand what fairies mean, it is helpful to look into the etymological origin of this term. *Fairy* comes from the French and is originally derived from the Latin *fata*, which means goddess of fate. In Middle High German the word was borrowed in the form *fei*, which is still visible in the verb *feien* (to make proof against) and the phrase *gefeit sein* (to be proof against). This is connected with a sense of being safeguarded. The fairies are thus associated with fate or destiny, like the Moirai or Parcae, who weave the threads of fate and cut them when they see fit. In general, however, fairies have a kindlier, less relentless quality to them. Good fairies bestow gifts; they reward people who treat them properly. In eastern and southern Europe, we still find the old belief that after the birth of a child, three wise women or natal goddesses appear and allot the child its destiny. But, just as with elves, one must get on their good side by offering them food and drink,[9] so children are protected through food offerings. We find an echo of this belief, in a Christianized form, in the custom of the baptismal meal at which the godfather and godmother are present.

It is an interesting question why, in myths and fairy tales, fate is for the most part connected with feminine figures. In Greek mythology, even Zeus, the father of the gods, has no power over the fate-spinning Moirai. They stand above his sphere of influence. Fate lies hidden in the darkness of Great Mother Nature, who assigns each person his lot and endows him with his natural potentialities. We also know how fate-determining earliest childhood is, when the baby, for better or worse, is completely at the mercy of the mother and her attitude. Here in the primal relationship, it is to a great extent determined whether later on the individual's sense of self and world will be grounded in a basic feeling of trust and confidence or mistrust and fear. For the baby, the mother is not yet a human being in her own right, distinguished emotionally from itself. But it experiences very existentially the contentment of being nurtured and protected or the intensive malaise of abandonment and fear. Though the mother relates personally to her own personal child, at the same time a natural maternal instinct, a general maternal way of perceiving and responding, is operative in her. The whole mother-child situation is archetypal; symbolically, it lies under the dominance of the Great Mother. At this point it becomes crucial how the personal mother relates to her own motherhood and thus to the child. Through conscious or unconscious rejection of the infant, and therefore of her own motherhood via a lack of mirroring, containing, or holding, she can, as it were, anger the mother goddess, who then revenges herself on the development of the child. Thus Erich Neumann writes: "The Great Mother Figure of the primal relationship is a goddess of fate who, by her favor or disfavor, decided over life and death, positive or negative development; and moreover, her attitude is the supreme judgment, so that her defection is identical with a nameless guilt on the part of the child." [10] Here he is alluding to the profound, often unfathomable guilt feelings we encounter in people with deeply disturbed primal relationships.

Through this, it becomes comprehensible why fate is left in feminine hands. Fairies, however, are friendly mother figures who are definitely accessible to human influence, that is, to the conscious attitude. If we are hospitable to them, let them enter, and pay heed to them, then they exercise a beneficial influence. Thus all this depends on our conscious relationship to these contents of the unconscious. Jung's guiding principle for psychotherapy is applicable here: "The only way to get at (the contents of the unconscious) in practice is to try to attain a conscious attitude which allows the unconscious to cooperate instead of being driven into opposition."[11]

In our tale, it is the thirteenth fairy who utters the curse. It should be noted that in the various versions of the Sleeping Beauty story, the number of fairies changes. Sometime we are told of seven invited fairies and of an eighth who for one reason or another is not invited. Sometimes, of three invited fairies, one becomes angry.[12] Here, however, I would like to stick with the Grimm's version of the tale and look into the psychological significance of the number symbolism of twelve and thirteen.[13] In superstition, thirteen is notorious as an unlucky number. Where does this actually come from? Twelve, determined by the archetypal numbers three and four, is a number that betokens wholesomeness, the dozen. A year requires twelve months for its completion, four seasons of three months each. In most of the ancient mysteries, twelve signified the twelve hours of the night or day and at the same time the twelve degrees of transformation, which were often represented by twelve robes. In this context, the thirteenth robe is the highest, definitive stage and represents the *solificatio* (becoming the sun), the realized mystical goal.[14] This thirteenth stage includes the previous twelve stages within it and thus really signifies the twelve as a unity, a whole. This is similar to the *quinta essentia*, which contains the four as a whole, as an "essence."

However, in another way, thirteen fails to be included in the order-related number twelve; it is an appendage, a leftover, something superfluous in the cosmos represented by twelve. With thirteen, one falls out of the cosmic order and into the realm of the chaotic and irrational, where things become uncontrollable and therefore often arouse fear and malaise. From the realm of the uncontrollable, anything can arise—fortune and misfortune both. For this reason, thirteen is also sometimes a lucky number. Both ways of interpreting the number thirteen—as the essence of twelve and as a token of chaos—might well play a role in the clarification of the course of events in our tale. There is no possibility of accommodating the dark, chaotic, irrational element in the kingdom. That is to say, in every conscious attitude, there is always something left out of account; the wholeness is never entirely in view. In our case, it is the thirteenth fairy, who in one way represents the dark, irrational element in nature and in another way the wholeness or unity of all natural-chthonic phenomena, the essence of all Mother Nature variants. When this fairy is not invited or taken into account, things shift out of balance, as can be seen from innumerable neuroses or distortions of civilized culture. At that point, the unconscious appears hostile, produces restrictive symptoms, takes revenge for being neglected precisely as the body takes revenge through illness for neglect of its needs. In our fairy tale, it is significant that the thirteenth fairy changes places, so to speak, with the twelfth, thus preserving the possibility of softening the whole situation. The thirteenth breaks into the order of the twelve and in this way at the last moment the negative element is forcibly taken up into the possibility of structured consciousness. In this way, the *whole* situation symbolized by the number thirteen is diminished in destructiveness. When one becomes conscious of the destructive aspects in oneself, they are not interpreted away. However, under certain circumstances, becoming conscious of them makes them somewhat less autonomous; they can no longer entirely take one over unexpectedly. In any case, this is a psychotherapeutic hope confirmed by many experiences. In no way can the curse be entirely undone; all the thirteenth as an expression of the wholeness of the twelve can do is soften it. Under no circumstances can a blessing or a curse be undone. Once it is uttered, it has its effect. In this connection, one might also think of the story of Isaac in the Old Testament, who unwittingly blesses his youngest son, Jacob, instead of his firstborn, Esau. The mistake cannot be rectified, because Isaac himself is not the master of blessing and curse.

One is thus compelled somehow to deal with the destructive

element in oneself consciously. The king in the fairy tale, however, provides a typical example of how not to deal with it: that is, through repression. His order was that all spindles in the kingdom should be burned. High up in the old tower, however, locked in with a rusty key, sits an enigmatic old woman whom the king's command has apparently not reached. Repression is seldom a felicitous solution for a problem; somewhere "in an upper room" it lingers—especially when it has to do with something as important as spinning. Spinning and weaving are typical womanly activities that play a role in numberless myths and fairy tales. In this regard, it is interesting that in the Middle Ages, the spindle was more or less the characteristic emblem of the German woman, while the sword was considered the sign of the German man. As a result, paternal relatives were called "sword relations" and maternal ones "spindle relations." [15] The sword symbolizes active confrontation—incisive, decisive, and precise Logos. In contrast, the spindle tends to connote more a sense of joining together, bringing into relationship, in other words, Eros. Fantasizing, including erotic fantasizing, is often thought of as spinning (as in "spinning yarns"). "Gretchen at the Spinning Wheel" is the name of one of the most beautiful love poems. [16]

Obviously, the equation of Logos with masculinity and Eros with feminity cannot be extended to men and women as concrete persons. Rather, Logos and Eros are basic principles of psychic life, both of which are at work in both sexes. [17]

Now, if all spindles, and with them the activity of spinning, are banned from the kingdom, that would signify, in psychological terms, the repression or suppression of fantasy and Eros (repression happens unconsciously; suppression is a conscious act). The child would have to be kept from her own spontaneous fantasies and impulses. We see this also, for example, in Pietism, where the view prevailed that human nature was bad, and children had to be kept from being natural and spontaneous and from playfully developing their fantasies. Children were shut up as much as possible, confined to working and praying, and were continually watched.[18] Any kind of spinning could be done only in dreams—in dreams, the little room of the old spinner lady up in the tower could not be subject to surveillance and control.

It is typical for the urge to spin to become overwhelming at the age of fifteen, as we find in our fairy tale. This is the age of sexual maturation. However, awakening sexuality with its concomitant fantasies works like poison if its eruption strikes a girl when she is completely unprepared. Here the old lady spinning above in the tower must be interpreted as a version of the evil fairy who uttered the curse and is now seeing to its realization. Psychologically, we can speak here of a negative mother complex, which often becomes acute in a situation such as this. Among other things, it is this negative mother complex that is often behind the compulsion young girls feel to inwardly reject their own awakening womanhood, to negate it, to try to do away with it. Thus it causes one to spin fantasies directed against one's own person, autonomous affect-laden fantasies of one's own inferiority. One's own existence in its natural unfolding cannot be treated with approval. Therefore, it is inconceivable that one could feel oneself taken seriously and approved of by a partner. Being pricked by the spindle thus means that the possibility of being a mature woman and "spinning" fantasies about men has a traumatic impact. The wound from the spindle means psychologically that erupting erotic fantasies and impulses bring on crippling fear. The sleeping state of Sleeping Beauty is clearly connected with the unawakened quality and the feelings of loneliness found in women caught in such a constellation. However, any attempt to get close to them emotionally is aggressively warded off. Thorns are driven into the flesh of any man who dares to approach. For example, sarcastic remarks ridiculing him and his manliness are used as a protection against the feared intimacy. The rose is after all the symbol of love and emotion. As is well known, however, there is no rose without thorns. The thorns symbolize the reverse side of loving devotion—wounding defense. Women with this problem themselves suffer from their thorns, as I have often noted in my practice. Their fear is stronger than they are. The king-father who has all the spindles burned lives on in them in the all-pervasive view that it is dangerous to let spinning fantasies and feelings arise. Often the dormant capacity for relationship is compensated for by greater professional diligence and efficiency; however, a great emptiness and loneliness, which is acknowledged as little as possible, becomes more and more pervasive as the brier hedge continues to grow.

A typical, often quite serious neurosis of young girls of this age is teenage anorexia nervosa. The girls refuse to eat, or if they manage to force themselves to eat something, they vomit it out. Menstruation ceases. One of the principal symptoms is a compulsion to lie; in other words, negative fantasies take the upper hand. The following is an example of teenage anorexia in which the underlying Sleeping Beauty constellation is quite evident. Our fairy tale describes in symbolic terms an archetypal background that can be the basis for a complex individual problem.

The fifteen-year-old girl whose case we shall consider was obliged to enter a psychiatric hospital. Hannah, as I shall call her, could not eat anymore. Though she wanted to, she had an insuperable resistance to it, a continuous absence of appetite. Every time she forced herself to eat, she had to vomit what she had eaten. At the time of entry into the hospital, she was already in an alarming, life-threatening condition of undernourishment and at first had to be artificially fed. After a few weeks, she became a bit stronger and was able to begin psychotherapy with me. She was outwardly friendly. However, as soon as I tried, out of therapeutic necessity, to become somewhat closer to her, I ran into a "brier hedge." Her defense consisted of sharp, aggressive complaints against the hospital and against her mother, sister, grandmother, and, on the first occasion, me as well. These complaints were uttered in very soft but penetrating, carping tones. She made her spikes and thorns clearly felt again and again. At the same time, she dreamed that she was languishing in a castle dungeon—an intensification of the Sleeping Beauty motif.

From her life history, the following elements were significant: from the beginning her parents had had a bad and extremely ambivalent marriage. The mother was still to a great extent bound to her own mother, the patient's grandmother. This grandmother had never been able to accept Hannah's father and tried to undermine her daughter's marriage. For his part, the father was never able to win over his mother-in-law. As a way out, he became involved in an extramarital relationship. This became grounds for divorce, and the mother moved with the patient and her younger sister into the grandmother's house. Thus the overpowerful world of the mother and grandmother was able to eliminate the father. The grandmother was very rich and spoiled the child terribly—but under the condition that she always be grateful, love the grandmother, and obey her. The mother, also dominated by the grandmother, was busy earning a living and did not see the child so often. As the child grew, it became ever clearer that she was beginning in many respects to resemble her father, who was greatly detested by her mother and grandmother. She was reproached with this at every turn. As a result, she felt herself more and more rejected and became terribly jealous of her younger sister, who was just like her mother. Thus the fateful evil fairy had cursed her with bearing the features of a father who seemed to embody evil and who was customarily referred to only in aggressive tones. But at the same time, Hannah began to spin fantasies about her father. The distant unknown father became the object of her secret longing—he would surely love her if she resembled him so much. But these fantasies were in turn the cause of guilt feelings. After all, they were forbidden. She would not have dared say such a thing to anyone. Her mother and grandmother would have become frightfully angry and repudiated her more than ever. What was "king" in this family was the unwritten law that in the primary interests of family harmony, no one could be allowed to have such fantasies. The spindle was thus banned from the kingdom.

When the patient was twelve years old, the mother remarried and, with her children, moved out of the grandmother's house. But the grandmother was unable to relinquish her power position. She continually claimed attention by means of her many gifts and fawning invitations. Since the new husband did not have a large income, the grandmother continually found opportunities to provide something for their household. In this way she hoped to reap gratitude and love and not to be shut out. As a result, there was still the feeling of being dependent on the grandmother. It should also be noted here that the patient's stay at the hospital and her psychotherapeutic treatment by me were paid for by the grandmother. Hannah and her stepfather got on quite well together. She secretly loved him, which is very understandable in the case of a father-craving like hers. All the while, the grandmother continued to make barbed remarks about the stepfather, who, she claimed, could not even feed his own family—which, by the way, was not at all the case. Thus for Hannah, it was a two-edged sword to love her stepfather, which, in a childlike and daughterly fashion, she did.

Then she entered early puberty, and it emerged that the stepfather was anything but insensitive to her burgeoning feminine charms. One day he made an explicit sexual advance to her, which triggered a trauma in her. She pricked herself on the spindle of her fantasies, which the stepfather had certainly unconsciously provoked. The old lady spinning in the tower, operative in the form of her personal grandmother, was thus proved right in her rejection of men. From this point on, Hannah began to lose her appetite and became ashamed of her womanly breasts. Also, typically, menstruation ceased. Her whole feminine instinctive world fell into a sleep like Sleeping Beauty's, which at the same time brought on depression and a dangerous level of life-negation.

After a few months of treatment and intensive psychotherapy in the psychiatric hospital, it began to look as though the first brier hedges were softening. Hannah gained weight, menstruation resumed, and in her dreams I could detect the beginnings of new life. But the grandmother came and, in "well-meaning" conversation, unconsciously sought to hinder such an awakening. During every visit, she would add up for Hannah the cost of the hospital stay and psychotherapy, making a point of how grateful Hannah should be to her self-sacrificing grandmother. Each time, this aroused the girl's resistance. This resistance came from what were in themselves healthy impulses toward autonomy and her desire to be no longer dependent on the grandmother. Yet at the same time they had a counterproductive effect in that they made her push to leave the clinic far too soon. Her family was glad to take her back; after all, the stay at the clinic was a bit of a disgrace. Although Hannah continued to come to psychotherapy as an out-patient, back in the old family milieu her symptoms took on new force. This in turn provided both mother and grandmother with a justification for repeatedly showing her that psychotherapy was futile. Every possible measure was taken by the overpowerful world of the mother and grandmother to extinguish the tiny spark of trust and confidence in the therapist that had begun to be kindled. When, a short time later, I moved into a new apartment, I was told that the trip back and forth was now too long for the daughter. Thus, just like Hannah's father and stepfather, I was eliminated by the negative mothers along with my therapeutic function. The therapeutic attempt at "redemption" got caught in the thorns of the brier hedge and "died a pitiful death," as the fairy tale says. The time for the girl to be redeemed seemed not to have come yet.[19]

But where there are thorns, there is also the possibility of blooming roses. They bloom for the prince who has the good fortune of arriving at the right time, after the end of the hundred-year curse. Obviously, these hundred years are not to be counted according to the conventional calendar, no more than was the eschatological "thousand-year Reich." The thousand-year Reich sunk into ruins and ashes after a bitter twelve years. Ten, one hundred, and one thousand are numbers that symbolize a totality. In superstition, a hundred years is almost always the length of time poor souls have to wait for anything. In addition, a day that a human being has to spend in the spirit world or the realm of the dead is said to be like a hundred years.[20] The element of time plays a key role in every process of human development, as in every natural process. Everything requires its due time. There is a Chinese legend about some farmers who had the idea of doing something about the slow growth of their rice plantations. They tugged on the plants every day in order to speed their growth—until the shoots finally died from uprooting. The long and slow quality of many an analytic process is also often bitterly decried. However, each person's hundred years can be of a different length, depending on the problem involved and his or her personal rhythm. Attempts at speeding things up run afoul of the brier hedge. The time must be ripe—and for ripening, nature requires its own time.

Every analyst knows that interpretations also need proper timing. The analyst must instinctively evaluate which interpretations the time is ripe for and which are still premature. By the same token, it frequently proves fruitless when people with psychic problems and fears are pushed into analysis by well-meaning friends or relatives, rather than deciding on their own to seek out an analyst. In these cases, the access to essential inner processes is often blocked for both analyst and analysand; the time for undertaking the difficult path of self-knowledge is not yet ripe.

On the whole, Sleeping Beauty is not a dramatic fairy tale. The heroine undergoes her fate passively, and the rescuing prince also does not really have to accomplish any heroic feat. Time is on his side. The way to the beautiful princess opens up as though by itself *at the right moment*. It is just a question of waiting for the right moment to come, which for certain obstructions in psychic development is sometimes the only option.

Apparently after the hundred years have elapsed, the pretraumatic condition is simply restored. The fairy tale describes this in complete detail—even to the cook, who finally fetches the kitchen boy the wallop he had set in motion a hundred years previous, hitting him "so hard that he howled." However, the fairy tale does not conclude merely with the restoration of the *status quo ante*. Something new has been added—the prince. In contrast to a purely medical treatment, which tries to restore a previous state of health, it is in the nature of a psychotherapeutic treatment that a cure can only lie in a new attitude of consciousness, which to a certain degree also entails personal maturation. Thus the emphasis in analytical psychotherapy lies not on restoration but on psychic transformation. For this reason, the medical categories of healing can never be completely applied to psychotherapy without violating the latter's autonomous laws.

Sleeping Beauty is liberated from her sleep state by the prince's kiss. But the prince is only able to redeem her because the time of the evil fairy and her curse is over and a new period is beginning. It is the beginning of a new approach to life—where there were previously thorns, roses have bloomed. Openness toward love has been established. The appearance of the prince also symbolizes the renewal of the "king," the possibility of a new attitude of consciousness that might come to "rule."

If we look at this denouement in terms of the psychotherapeutic process, the new attitude is connected with the loving acceptance of one's own womanhood, on which ultimately any capacity for love must be based. If all goes well, this "awakening" takes place when the genuine affection and appreciation of the analyst becomes the patient's own inner attitude. After all, the period of the curse was characterized by negative fantasies directed against one's own person having their crippling and isolating effect. Now the gift of the good fairies can bear fruit—the unfolding of one's given potential is no longer obstructed.

The blockage of life flow symbolized by the initial sterility of the royal couple has now been overcome. The princess celebrates her marriage to the prince and they live "happily to the end of their lives." In the reality of human life, the end of such a "happy life" usually must come fairly quickly if the old sterility is not to reassert itself on some new level. For "as long as one continues to develop, inner peace, even for those whose lives have been enriched by an encounter with the unconscious, is only a breathing space between the conflict solved and the conflict to come, between answers and questions that throw us into turmoil and suffering, until new insights or new transformations bring a fresh solution and the inner and outer space are once again reconciled."[21]

NOTES

1. Mario Jacoby, "Sinn und Unsinn des Leidens," in *Leiden* (publication of the C. G. Jung Institute, Zurich), vol. 20 (1976), pp. 36–53.
2. This essay was originally published in 1978. —Editor
3. See the chapter "C. G. Jung's View of Fairy Tale Interpretation" in Part One.
4. Erich Neumann, "Der Mond und das matriarchale Bewusstsein," in *Zur Psychologie des Weiblichen* (On the Psychology of the Feminine) (Zurich: Rascher, 1953), pp. 67ff.
5. C. G. Jung, *Collected Works*, vol. 8 (Princeton: Princeton University Press).
6. Mario Jacoby, "Das Tier im Traum," in *Instinkte und Archetypen im Verhalten der Tiere und im Erleben der Menschen* (Darmstadt: Wissenschaftliche Buchgesellschaft, 1976), p. 312.
7. Marie-Louise von Franz, *Problems of the Feminine in Fairy Tales* (Dallas: Spring Publications, 1972), p. 24.
8. Erich Neumann, *The Great Mother: An Analysis of the Archetype* (Princeton, N.J.: Princeton University Press, 1972).
9. Hedwig von Beit, *Symbolik des Märchens* (Bern: Franke, 1960), p. 695.

10. Erich Neumann, *The Child* (Boston: Shambhala Publications, 1990), p. 87.

11. Jung, CW 16.

12. J. Bolte and G. Povlika, *Anmerkungen zu den Kinder- und Hausmärchen der Brüder Grimm*, vol. 1 (Hildesheim: Olms, 1963), p. 435.

13. See also the symbolic interpretation of thirteen in Ingrid Riedel's chapter, "The Smith's Daughter Who Knew How to Hold Her Tongue."

14. Von Beit, *Symbolik des Märchens*, vol. 1, p. 699.

15. H. Bächtold-Stäubli, *Handwörterbuch des deutschen Aberglaubens*, vol. 8 (Berlin and Leipzig: de Gruyter, 1936), p. 263.

16. Johann Wolfgang von Goethe, *Faust* (part 1).

17. See the discussion on Logos and Eros in the next chapter, "The Witch in Dreams, Complexes, and Fairy Tales."

18. H. Reble, *Geschichte der Pädagogik* (Stuttgart: Klett, 1962), p. 117.

19. The effect of the Sleeping Beauty motif in the psychic life of a man is shown in the preceding chapter, "Bewitchment and Liberation."

20. Bächtold-Stäubli, *Handwörterbuch des deutschen Aberglaubens*, vol. 4, pp. 598ff.

21. Aniela Jaffé, *The Myth of Meaning in the Work of C. G. Jung* (London: Hodder and Stoughton, 1970), p. 56.

MARIO JACOBY

The Witch in Dreams, Complexes, and Fairy Tales

The Dark Feminine in Psychotherapy

Through looking at a young man's mother complex and two witch dreams—one from the masculine perspective and one from the feminine—it becomes clear what the witch constellation looks like on an inner psychic level. In the man's negative mother complex, the witch shows herself as the overpowering feminine principle that devours his development toward independence and renders him incapable of relationship. A comparison with ideas from Malleus Maleficarum, The Hammer of Witches, *shows how, during the witch persecutions, negative aspects of the mother archetype were ascribed to individual women, who were thus made to bear the projection of masculine fears. Christianity brought on a split in the mother archetype. The mother archetype's dark aspect was repressed and appeared instead in a compensatory fashion and as a cultural undercurrent in fairy tales. In a patient's dream, the archetype appears as the "mistress of the animals," by whom the anima figure of the man is torn to pieces. How the disengagement of the anima from the mother image can finally be achieved is shown by further dreams containing fairy tale motifs.*

A young man came to my office, very distraught. The following problems were harrying him. For about two years, he had been having a relationship with a woman who was about ten years older than he was. He had maintained his own apartment but for the most part was living with this woman. Though feeling the pangs of a guilty conscience, he had recently moved back into his own apartment and left his girlfriend to live by herself. When from time to time he tried to indicate his need to be alone, she accused him of being incapable of relationship. But at the same time, in his girlfriend's apartment, he felt so blocked from performing the creative work that he needed for his artistic profession that he was desperate. He was unable to work in her apartment when she was there, and at home in his own place he could not work because of guilt over having left her alone.

This has the familiar sound of the excuses of so-called "unrecognized geniuses": "The brilliant things I could do if only . . ." If only, for example, this woman would leave me alone. But with this young man, such suspicions were unfounded, since he already had certain genuine achievements in his field behind him. He was thus in the throes of a real crisis, in a state of panic over having become impotent and sterile in his artistic development and in his profession. He also indicated that this problem was not confined to his professional activity; sexually also, a disturbing impotence was developing. According to him, his girlfriend's relationship to the body was far more solidly intact than his, and this intensified his own inhibitions and fears. As a result he felt in the wrong, felt that he was failing to supply something essential that she was entitled to and that he was thus in her debt. He did not feel himself man enough to discharge this debt. Instead, he promised to fulfill a long-cherished career wish of hers, which was possible for him because of family connections. His girlfriend had staked her entire professional future on this and was now waiting for him to keep his promise. For him, this meant that this woman would now become more deeply involved in his own life while fundamentally he wanted to be free of her. He was coming to hate her more and more, and these hate impulses were intensifying his sense of guilt.

What a weakling, what a good-for-nothing, how incapable of relationship he was! These were the accusations he leveled against
himself. He wanted and had to get rid of this woman at any price,
otherwise his future success was blocked. Yet he dared not do this.
Every time he tried to talk to her about it, she managed to con-
vince him of his guilt and inadequacy.

To myself I thought: this is tantamount to bewitchment; it is
as though this woman has him under a witch's spell. What I said
to him was: "The basic problem, it seems to me, is that in this
woman's presence you lose your connection with yourself. You
become alienated from yourself and doubt that you can really rely
on your own thoughts, impulses, and feelings."

So I mentioned nothing of my "bewitchment" diagnosis. After all, it was far from presentable in scientific terms; it sounded
more like something from the Middle Ages than a sophisticated
neuropsychological diagnosis. All the same, I was not ashamed of
my naive fantasy in reaction to his story; on the contrary, I found
it quite vivid and meaningful. But at this moment he could not be
told about it, because it might lead to misunderstandings. *Witch*
and *bewitchment* are words capable even today of constellating
many emotion-laden associations. We have only to think of China,
where Mao Zedong's widow, Jiang Qing, was declared a witch and
was to be "boiled in oil" along with her helpers. Also their "dogs'
heads" were to be "smashed." In any case, the effect of the word
bewitched is different from that of a Latin technical term of scientific diagnosis. And there was something else that was critical
for me: I wanted to avoid having the young man, with his courage
boosted by me, go now to the woman and accuse her of being a
witch. Even though it might be the case that she had "hexed" him
into impotence and self-alienation, this could only have happened
because he had unconsciously imbued her with the power to do
so. In other words, the witchlike qualities had been projected onto
her. The great sorceress and magic-wielding witch is an arche-

typal image that must have been active within him. His girl-friend's instinctively surehanded exploitation of this weakness is quite common for this type of relationship.

It also came out in my conversations with him that this girl-friend strikingly resembled his mother. His mother had spoiled him badly, like the witch in "Hansel and Gretel," letting him nibble on her gingerbread house in order to lure him inside. She had felt the need to keep her darling little son dependent on her. She had taken him under her wing and dominated him on into early manhood by forestalling all his independent steps, always knowing better and arranging his life for him. Thus the overpow-ering feminine principle was constellated in him, devouring his urge for autonomy, castrating his manhood. As a result, in spite of being thirty and in spite of his good intellectual development, emotionally he had remained a child, a "momma's boy." He was seeking his mother again in his female partner, but could live nei-ther with her nor without her. He was really bewitched.

I have presented this as a typical example of how the witch figure can have its effect in the psychic realm. Psychologically, as already mentioned, the witch is to be regarded as an archetypal image. That is to say, she symbolizes typical potentialities of hu-man experience. These are primarily fearsome experiences of be-ing overwhelmed by something unwanted, emotions being ex-perienced as hostile to the ego. In relation to them, the ego experiences itself as a helpless victim of overpowering emotions and affects, feels constrained, possessed, or emptied out, alienated from itself—expressed mythologically, bewitched. Many great di-vine sorceresses are known from ancient mythology. There is the famous Circe, daughter of the sun god Helios, who changed men into pigs. There is the Gorgon Medusa with her hair of snakes, whose glance turned men to stone. Artemis transformed Actaeon into a stag because he saw her bathing naked, and as a result he was torn to pieces by his own hunting dogs. Each of these examples involves dehumanization, being turned into an animal or into stone, that is, self-alienation and loss of identity.

Our specific Western conception of a witch, which I shall now examine more closely, derives from medieval times. Its specific meaning was developed by the theology of those times, which laid the groundwork for the great witch persecutions and trials. Etymologically, the German word for witch, *Hexe*, is thought to be connected to the German substantive *Hag*, meaning fence, edge, enclosure. This is connected to the English word *hag*, meaning an ugly or monstrous old woman. In accordance with this etymology, a witch would be a demonic being dwelling on fences or hedges, in fact a "fence rider," or "fence woman."[1] This derivation seems to me highly significant. A hedge or fence marks a borderline. Thus the witch would be a creature of the border region between the human and the demonic—psychologically, between the realm of consciousness and the unconscious. In a Swedish law from around 1170, for the first time we find mention of troll-like women with loose hair riding on fence poles. Later, as we know, witches were said to ride broomsticks to Brocken Mountain, the site of the Walpurgis Night witch's sabbath. This is also a description of a magical journey from one realm to another. If we survey the oldest references to witches and related figures, we find three characterizations: (1) a man-eating being, (2) a slovenly, loose (in all senses) female, and (3) a clown or actor. The third meaning becomes relevant to our context if we consider that an actor is a master of transformation, who can enchant himself and his audience through the use of masks. For primitive man, the portrayer of demons is at the same time the demon itself.[2]

Around 1486, toward the end of the Middle Ages, the notorious *Malleus Maleficarum* (*The Hammer of Witches*) appeared, a document composed by two Dominican monks.[3] It contained as a preface a papal bull of Innocent VIII, which lent it the weight it required to serve as the basis for the witch persecutions of the

Inquisition. In this ill-fated document, a variety of different notions about the nature of witches are connected together. The witch (1) has a pact with the devil as well as being in an amorous relationship with him; (2) promotes heresy, that is, the worship of strange gods; (3) practices harmful black magic; and (4) flies through the air and transforms herself into animal form.

The first two points are essentially derived from medieval theology, whereas the third and forth points are based on old folk beliefs of various peoples. Especially striking in this document is the extensive treatment of the sexual theme going hand in hand with a crude repudiation of women. For example, we read the following in the *The Hammer of Witches* about the nature of women:

> By woman is understood craving of the flesh, in accordance with the saying, "I found woman bitterer than death, and even a good woman is subjected to the craving of the flesh." Women are superstitious in greater numbers than men, because they are gullible, because by nature, on account of the fluidity of their complexion, they are easier to influence toward receptivity to inspirations brought about by the impression of separate spirits; because their tongue is slippery, and because they are scarcely able to conceal from their cronies what they have learned through vile art; and, since they have no strength, they readily seek to revenge themselves in secret through witchery. Since they are deficient in all faculties of the soul as of the body, it is no wonder that they bring more evil deeds to bear against those with whom they competitively strive. . . . These deficiencies are also indicated by the creation of the first woman, in that she was formed from a crooked rib. . . . It is also made clear in regard to the first woman that by nature they have less faith . . . which is also expressed in the etymology of the word: the word *femina* comes from *fe* meaning *fides*, faith, and *minus* meaning less. Thus the *femina* is she who has less faith.[4]

As we see, this is "etymology" in the service of emotional prejudices! Now let us hear something about the iniquities of the witches:

> They practice sexual orgies with the incubus, the imp lover. . . . That is to say that although the incubus is visible to the witches, it is not so for bystanders. But they have frequently seen witches lying on their backs in fields or in the forest, their sexual parts exposed, their limbs disposed in the manner of those obscenities, with arms and thighs working; while the incubus remained invisible for the bystanders, at the end of the act an extremely black vapor the length of a man might rise up from the witch into the air, but only rarely.

Whether or not there is anything true in such descriptions of the behavior of so-called witches, they also correspond to an attack of grand hysteria as diagnosed and described by the Parisian neurologist Charcot at the end of the last century. Eugen Bleuler also called attention in his psychiatric textbook to this phenomenon, in which, in the famous *arc de cercle*, orgasm-like spasms took place.[6] Today, grand hysteria with this symptomatology seems to have pretty well disappeared.

In our document witches are also accused of using sorcery to inflame people's hearts with excessive love, of inhibiting fertility, removing the male member, using arts of illusion to turn people into animals, bringing about premature birth, and sacrificing children to the demons.[7] "The removal of the male sexual member takes place through the deceptive trickery of the demons in the ways mentioned, by perturbation of the organ of sight in that the sensory shapes connected with the faculty of representation are transformed."[8] What this is telling us, in other words, is that the organ of sight is deceiving itself when it continues to find the spirited-away penis in the usual place.

As we see, the entire arsenal of the imaginary world that is bound up with the archetype of the terrible goddess is foisted off here on poor individual women. They bear the projections of masculine fears of being overwhelmed by uncontrollable instinctual drives and of ego loss. The fear of castration discovered by Freud in our century was also clearly in play here, and compensation for it was sought in the witch persecutions. Under certain circumstances, the witch is also supposed to have power over conception, birth, and children. Psychologically, on a symbolic level, this could mean blockage and sterilization of creativity in its broadest sense—something the young man we mentioned initially was suffering from.

As antidotes for witchery, *The Hammer of Witches* recommends confession, pilgrimage, making the sign of the cross, pious prayers, communion, benediction, verbal formulas, holy water, being rebaptized, and so forth. However, the last recourse of the church was the extermination of witches, which it was obligated to by divine commandment.

How are we to understand this ghastly mass madness psychologically? One possible hypothesis is the following: Like every archetype, the primordial image of the great feminine has its double aspect. Since the Great Feminine or Great Mother is a symbol of a very multifaceted human experience, its meaning cannot be sharply delineated in discursive terms. We might perhaps say that it is the experience of connectedness or relatedness to or indeed of dependency on "Nature," as we refer to it in the broadest sense. In connection with the archetype of the Great Mother, Jung often spoke of Eros as contrasted to the primordial image of the wise old man / demonic father, which has the quality of Logos. Thus Eros means relatedness to natural being both in and around us. Instincts, impulses, feelings, and intuitions are its psychic functions. Logos represents the possibility of differentiation between subject and object for the sake of knowledge and intellectual penetration. We may want to judge something "objectively," but our emotional relationship to it gets in the way.

Both love and hate have the tendency to make us blind to the true nature of other people. Logos, with its power of discrimination, also involves a critical attitude (from the Greek *krinein*, to discriminate or distinguish). Are the things of nature good as they are or could they, indeed should they, be otherwise? Human technology capable of altering nature and rendering it useful is ultimately based on Logos, just as are ethical laws. The latter are judgmental—condemnatory guidelines and norms concerning how human beings ought to behave—often in contrast to how they actually do behave according to their nature.

These two comprehensive basic elements of human existence—the father and mother archetypes, Logos and Eros—are often in conflict with one another. At the same time, each contains within itself a variety of conflicting aspects. In any case, the double-sided quality, with the paired aspects of positive-negative, above-below, helpful-destructive, good-evil, light-dark, is very striking. The more archaic the symbolic representation is, the less differentiated and more ambiguous its impact. The ancient mother deities are both protective and destructive. There are goddesses who bring about sensual-sexual-orgiastic experience with all its dangers—Aphrodite and Ishtar are examples of this. But there is also Sophia, the goddess of wisdom, or the owl-eyed Athena, who can see in the dark. With the advent of Christianity, an ever greater split appeared in the psychic effects of the archetype. The only legitimate figure corresponding to the archetype of the Great Feminine became Mary, Mother of God. But she represents only heavenly, sublimated love and never comes in contact with earthy sexuality; she bears her son in everlasting virginity. Of course, a miraculous birth is always part of the myth of the divine child. For example, the Egyptian Isis conceived her son Horus by means of a ritual phallus. Nevertheless it is striking that the earthy-physical and ecstatic-passionate aspects of human nature are excluded from the image of Mary. Thus the archetype of the great feminine was split in such a way that the dark side lost the status of divinity that it possessed in ancient times. Nonetheless this aspect continued to be active, but in despised, condemned, and therefore all the more fascinating domains. The dark feminine degenerated into a witch who is the devil's lover. It is a plausible hypothesis that the archaic male fellowship, out of which, with time, the strict patriarchal societal order developed, was actually a defense against the overpowering great feminine, which was projected onto women. On the whole, the greater one's own unconsciousness and repression, the stronger the projection. All the impulses from the unconscious that are not in conformity with the ego's intentions are off-loaded onto the environment. The witches are the guilty ones!

Also, on a purely practical level, we must not forget that every man has at one time experienced himself as dependent upon the overpowering feminine—his own mother. Ultimately he also feels himself at the mercy of the overpowering unconscious within himself, although this is often denied. The emotional element, to the extent that it opposes the intentions and dignity of the ego with its restlessness, fears, and impulses, must be warded off. The attempt to be master in one's own inner house appears at the same time in projected form. The woman must be the object of the man's dominance and control in order for him to experience himself as strong and masculine. In my opinion, genuine partnership between the sexes becomes possible only when this defensive posture vis-à-vis the unconscious begins to lose its rigidity. This is a broad and complex problem of the collective patriarchal outlook which every school of depth psychology must come to grips with in its own way.

In any case, the witch as an archetypal image symbolizes a threat to ego-consciousness and its development. Expressed in the modern idiom, she is an image for the development-inhibiting mother complex. For this reason, in fairy tales she is often connected with the stepmother and sometimes she is identified with her—I am thinking of "Snow White" (Grimm's no. 53) and

"Little Brother and Little Sister" (Grimm's no. 11). She changes herself into the wolf who has devoured the kindly grandmother (who equals the Great Mother) in "Little Red Riding Hood" (Grimm's no. 26). She spins her web of fate in the upper room of the tower in "Sleeping Beauty" (Grimm's no. 50). She keeps Hansel and Gretel prisoner in order to eat them up (Grimm's no. 15). She shuts up Rapunzel in a high tower (Grimm's no. 12); she turns Jorinda into a nightingale (Grimm's no. 69); and in "The Golden Children" (Grimm's no. 85), one of the brothers is turned into stone. She gives poisoned potions and creates ruinous temptations. In Russian fairy tales, the witch Baba Yaga is precisely depicted in her grisly abundance of power. The fence of her house is made out of human bones and on the fence posts are human skulls. The gate hinges are human feet, the bolt a human hand, and the lock a human mouth with sharp teeth. Baba Yaga has a broom with which she can instantly wipe out her tracks. At her service are the three horsemen Bright Day, Red Sun, and Black Night. It is striking that nonetheless she is not unequivocally evil and destructive—sometimes, as one endowed with profound knowledge, she shows the way (as, for example, in the Russian fairy tale "The Frog Princess"). In "Vasilisa the Beautiful," it is finally the skull from Baba Yaga's fence that burns up the evil stepmother and her daughters with its light. The Russian Baba Yaga seems to represent the archetype of the dark feminine in a more comprehensive fashion than purely as the destructive witch. In Russian tales where the witch crops up as part of motifs parallel to the German Grimm's tales, she is often characterized as an evil woman who nevertheless possesses magical powers.

Of course witches and being bewitched play a major role, in a more or less clear form, in dreams. I can provide an example of this from the analysis of a thirty-year-old man. The dream is as follows:

> I am in a gigantic castlelike house. There is a woman owner who has lots of servants and a chambermaid. The woman

has nothing to do and spends her day idly or playing cards. She possesses a gigantic dog that she has trained strictly and that does everything she says. The chambermaid is more or less forcing herself on a young man in the house. The mistress of the house, however, also seems to like this man. They play lots of games in which the mistress of the house bullies the maid and tries to put her at a disadvantage. However, the maid always skillfully eludes the trap. For this reason, the mistress of the house resolves to bring about her downfall. She calls her dog and jams her finger in its mouth all the way to the back of its fangs, then sets the dog on the maid. I'm terribly afraid of the dog for myself as well, thinking it might mistakenly attack me too. So I say to the mistress of the house that she should stay by me, since her presence seems to provide protection from the dog. But she replies that the dog only does exactly what she orders it to do. Now I hear a dog yelping; the light goes out, and I am in a gigantic dark room. I believe I am already being pursued by this dog, but in the midst of this immense fear, at the same time I have the feeling that I simply have to yield to my fate. This scene is now over. The mistress of the house calls me and tells me coldbloodedly that the maid is dead now, torn apart by the dog, and the young man also no longer means anything to her. During the meal, she recounts in complete detail how the dog tore the maid to pieces. I can't listen anymore and ask her to change the subject. I think about how I would like to get out of this house where so many bad things happen. At the same time, I'm afraid that then she would set the dog on me as well. At that moment, there is a knock at the door downstairs and a man's voice calls up that he wants to speak to the mistress of the house concerning the death of this maid. Relieved, I think: she is not so all-powerful after all; it seems she still has to answer for what she does.

In this dream, the destructive feminine principle appears as the mistress of animals. Like the hellhound Cerberus, her dog also seems to keep watch to prevent anyone from escaping her sphere of power. The dog was also the companion animal of the underworld goddess Hecate as well as the animal sacred to Artemis. For her sake, as already mentioned, Actaeon was torn to pieces by dogs.

The dreamer had in reality experienced his mother as the jealous tyrant of the house. By this time, he was externally independent of this mother; he visited her only rarely and was critical of her. But in his inner experience she continued to deprive him of his freedom, because through her the archetypal image of the terrible mother was constellated; she remained dominant in the psychic household of this young man. Thus it was his current psychic state that was represented and experienced in the dream in an archetypal way.

Unfortunately, in the present framework I can only touch briefly upon the main outlines of the dream events. We have the motif of jealousy between the mistress and the servant girl. This motif plays a major role in many fairy tales, often taking the form of a stepmother's envy of her stepdaughter's beauty. The classic example is "Snow White" (Grimm's no. 53). We also think of Venus's envy of Psyche in Apuleius's tale of Amor and Psyche. The killing of the stepdaughter by some magical means is the usual next step. In our dream, the maid is torn to pieces by the mistress's dog. This could have the following meaning in terms of masculine experience: if we apply the notions of Jungian psychology here, the maid would be a so-called *anima* figure. *Anima*, "soul," is what Jung called the image of the feminine in the masculine psyche. It is the "eternal feminine," which animates and inspires him. Projection of the anima on a woman usually results in a spellbound falling in love. On the inner psychic level, the anima signifies the potentiality for being in touch with one's "soul," which tends in the course of masculine ego development to be denied and repressed as too weak, too effeminate, too unmanly. The anima then manifests via the back way, as it were, in the form of sentimentality, moodiness, and obsessive states. Since in Jung's time, the images of masculine and feminine were relatively sharply delineated and not in doubt, he also referred to a man's feminine traits as the anima. Our views of what is masculine and what is feminine are in flux today. Furthermore, the idea that the functions of animus and anima are operative in both sexes is gaining ground. But all the same, Jung's psychology of anima and animus made him a pioneer of modern ideas of emancipation.[9] Anima and animus, with their opposite-gender traits and tendencies, counteract complete identification with socially accepted gender roles.

The anima, clearly, develops and differentiates itself out of the primordial mother image. Jung, however, never precisely investigated and described this development and differentiation. In the work of Erich Neumann we find some initial sketches of this, but on the whole not very much work has been done in this area. In any case, one thing is sure: fixation on the mother image hinders the differentiation of the anima. The mother continues to dominate, and no girl (or maid) has a real chance. This is the constellation that is depicted in the above dream. The mistress keeps jealous watch to make sure that no one but her has a chance with the masculine element. What was the practical effect of this on our young man? His relations with the female sex were unstable. He tended to seek out motherly partners out of a need above all to be accepted and understood. (Even in the dream he seeks protection from the mistress of the house.) This worked well enough for short periods, during which his inner anima noticeably became alive. But then suddenly, out of a clear blue sky, his girlfriends would begin to really get on his nerves. This often went hand in hand with sexual impotence. Experiencing resistance, he would sniff out whatever negative things he could about the girl and tear to pieces bit by bit everything she had meant to him. In this way, his mistress's dog did its work—his inner mother image was, so to speak, jealous and let loose her dog to destroy the relationship. But imprisonment by the mistress of the house and her keen-nosed hound also manifested on the inner psychic level. The young man became very namby-pamby and passive. A short time after he committed himself to anything and began to feel the animated inner forces of the self, an inner tearing to pieces began to take place. He would relentlessly get on the track of his own weaknesses and inadequacies and fall into despondency and depression. He also projected the keen-nosed dog on the outside; that is, suddenly he could feel himself being unfavorably observed by other people who seemed to sniff out his weak points. Thus his relationship to himself (anima) was torn to pieces and he let himself be crippled by destructive doubts.

The sphere of power of the mistress of the house within himself had become all-pervasive. But at the end of the dream, she was called to answer for her deeds by a male voice unknown to the dreamer. We might well think here of the male analyst and the effect of analysis. However, the analyst can produce a result only if there is an inner willingness in the analysand himself, that is, if the analytical relationship proves capable of constellating helpful inner tendencies. This male voice calling for the facing of responsibility is thus at the same time the father archetype in the analysand coming to the fore. In my analysand's actual life, his father had been a weak figure who was simply set aside as a model for identification and constellation. Thus the maternal power sphere was one-sidedly hypertrophied. In the analysis, the hitherto only latent paternal element began to come to life. It is interesting in the present context that a year later my analysand had a dream in which he experienced forcefully and skillfully taking a daughter away from a mother and afterward dancing with her. The disengagement of the anima from the mother image was gradually accomplished thanks to the growing strength of the ego. This motif, too, is often represented in fairy tales as the liberation of the daughter from the clutches of the witch-mother through the love of a prince. Examples of this from the Grimm's tales are "Rapunzel," "Jorinda and Joringel," and "Snow White."

Of course the witch also plays a role in the feminine psyche.

As an appropriate example of the impact of the witch in the feminine psyche, I would like to present the dream of a twenty-five-year-old female analysand:

> This happens in the Middle Ages. I and a girl are in a valley in the mountains together. Bewitched cows are in charge of everything, and we ourselves are bewitched. I am now suddenly grabbed by a bewitched cow and dragged along with her. Everything is dark, and we are going through dark valleys. But I know that the only way to get free is to let myself be dragged along by the bewitched cow. The cow drags me into a village where a theater stage is standing. I am dragged onto this stage, and there the cow changes into a nice, very fatherly man. I am supposed to dance with him, and he shows me various dance steps. I think: But I can't do that. Music sounds, and as it does I dare to try one of the steps and then keep on dancing. I know that I will be released as soon as the music is over.

Here the witch does not herself appear as a figure, but exercises her power through the bewitched cows that rule the valley. As concerns the life history of my analysand, it should be mentioned that her mother was caught up in a medieval-like Catholicism that was used to substantiate and justify her own depression. According to this, the earth was a vale of tears, humanity with its instinctual nature was under the sway of original sin, and penitence and continual prayer were the only way to God's favor. She raised my analysand with this outlook. No wonder the dream took place in the Middle Ages. Instinctive milk- and warmth-providing motherliness (symbolized by the cows) is experienced as bewitched. That which is satisfying and pleasant—one's own instinctive impulses—cannot be trusted; all of that is dangerous and sacrilegious. My analysand's basic problem was that she was afraid to relate to herself, felt obliged to reject her own nature, was ashamed of her every manifestation, and experienced herself as guilty and inferior. Thus she felt herself to be "bewitched." She associated the girl who was with her in the dream with a schoolmate who was rejected by everyone—an image of her own rejectedness. On top of everything, the mother had bound the girl to her in a possessive fashion and found ways to undermine any affection she might have felt for her father, which was necessary for healthy development. At the time of the beginning of the analysis, the analysand was entirely dependent on her as the mother who always knew better.

In the dream, the masculine-paternal principle also appears as a bewitched cow but then changes into its true shape. It changes because the analysand, in spite of her fear, is able to accept being dragged along as an ultimately freeing experience. This theme can only be understood in connection with what was going on in the analysis. The fatherly man who appeared out of the bewitched cow reminded her of me, the analyst. Transference here was of the utmost importance for the therapy. Being dragged along meant trustfully abandoning herself to the overpowering course of events. Initially in the analysis she was full of ambivalence and fear, expecting me to take her to task directly, berate and ridicule her the way her mother did. At the same time, in her imagination I was the wise and understanding ideal father from whom she sought support. Such impulses were despicable in her eyes, wicked and witchlike—after all, her mother had succeeded in undermining her affection for her father. For that reason, the image of the paternal-masculine was also bewitched. If the tiniest impulse of feeling for me emerged during an analytic session, she had to punish herself for it afterward. Punishment consisted in forbidding herself to think about me. This isolated her terribly and continually "castrated" the efficacy of the therapy. Moreover, although she felt I was able to understand and accept much of what she said, she feared that "in reality" I also would find her ridiculous. After the sessions she would feel ashamed about all the "impossible junk" she had said to me and expected me to scold her or ridicule her for it in the next session—which is apparently what her mother did, in her ongoing moodiness. Thus it was extremely difficult for her to perceive and accept my empathy and affective attunement to her way of being, which is what we find expressed in her dream image of the dancing and the music. The dissolution of the bewitchment occurs in the dream through surrender and the ability to accept her own problem without her self-esteem being destroyed in the process. Learning to accept herself as an integral being with both light and dark sides was the most difficult task for my analysand. Attempts to take an accepting attitude toward herself were continually attacked by the "witch," and the result was an overwhelming mood of depression with the basic feeling of having no "birthright," no right to exist.

Dealing with the witch and overcoming her destructiveness is on the whole the theme of most fairy tales in which she appears. Although she is powerful, her sphere of power is limited. There are forces that are capable of coping with her and that, under certain conditions, are superior to her. Though in "Hansel and Gretel" it is the children's alert trickery that defeats her, very often it is love that is stronger than the destructiveness of the witch. We need only think of "Rapunzel," where the prince, blinded by the witch, is made to see again through his beloved's tears. The love of the king's son in "Snow White" is stronger than the witch's death plan. In "Jorinda and Joringel," it is the red flower that exorcises the witch's power. In "Vasilisa the Beautiful," Baba Yaga is unable to bear the blessing of the good mother. In "The Golden Children," the spell that turns one of the brothers to stone can be undone through the other brother's threatening the witch from a distance with his rifle.

In many fairy tales, the witch is burned. She must always be combated and overcome for the action to proceed further in a living way. That is the archetypal requirement of the human maturation process. Things go badly if this archetypal requirement is projected onto other people and made a matter of concrete action, as in the case of the medieval witch burnings. However, in the matter of overcoming regressive, fixated psychic tendencies with their fascination and horror, burning symbolizes the fact that this process of overcoming is bound up with many emotions. No one really feels at ease when the witch's true face makes its appearance. The spellhas to be overcome by mobilizing all possible resources. As we know, the witch plays an important role for every child. Whenever the essentially well-adjusted real mother is excessive in her care and obstructs the independence process through overattachment, she is unconsciously experienced as a devouring witch. But often the child's own regressive needs also have something frightening about them and show up in the child's play and fantasies in the form of a witch. The really attuned mother is not too frightened, nor does she feel too narcissistically hurt when her children try to free themselves from her through defiance and other manifestations. For when she tries to pit herself against these bids for freedom, she becomes a witch.

The witch as a symbol of the devouring feminine thus occupies an important place, despite her dangerous traits, in the psychic household as a whole. It is precisely her threatening quality that mobilizes the forces that can overcome her, which is usually described in fairy tales as a major gain. The psychic crisis she brings on spurs us to new awareness and to efforts in the direction of living progression. As is well known, maturation cannot take place without difficulties and without profound experiential knowledge concerning the vulnerability of all that is human. However, this should not be construed as denying that in many cases the "bewitched" condition cannot be overcome in its manifestation as neurosis or even psychosis. This is where the psychotherapist comes in. Whether or not he or she can free the patient from the clutches of the witch depends on very many factors. Ultimately, this is only possible with God's help—*deo concedente*, as the alchemists used to say.

NOTES

1. "Etymologie," *Der Grosse Duden* (Mannheim: Bibliographisches Institut, 1963).
2. H. Bächtold-Stäubli, "Hexe," in *Handwörterbuch des deutschen Aberglaubens* (Berlin and Leipzig: de Gruyter, 1930/31).
3. J. Sprenger and H. Institoris, *Der Hexenhammer*, translated by J. W. Schmidt (Berlin: Barsdorf Verlag, 1906).
4. Ibid., vol. 1, pp. 97ff.
5. Ibid., vol. 2, p. 67.
6. Eugen Bleuler, *Lehrbuch der Psychiatrie*, 8th ed. by Manfred Bleuler (Berlin, 1949), p. 379.
7. Sprenger and Institoris, *Der Hexenhammer*, vol. 1, p. 106.
8. Ibid., vol. 2, p. 86.
9. See James Hillman, "Anima," in *Spring* (1973), pp. 97–132; Verena Kast, *The Nature of Loving: Patterns of Human Relationship* (Wilmette, Ill.: Chiron Publications, 1986), pp. 89–98.

Index of Fairy Tales